Parts o

Control box   Title bar

Radio button   Spin button

Command button

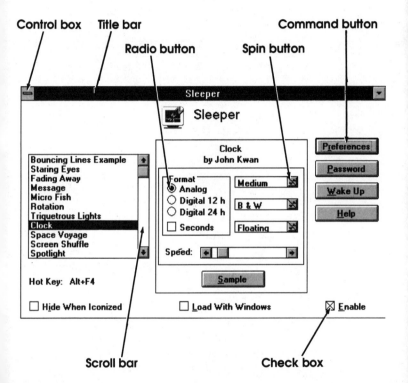

Scroll bar   Check box

The Sybex Instant Reference Series

Instant References are available on these topics:

AutoCAD Release 11

dBASE

dBASE III PLUS Programming

dBASE IV Programming

dBASE IV 1.1

DESQview

DOS

DOS 5

Hard Disk

Harvard Graphics

Harvard Graphics 3

Lotus 1-2-3 Release 2.2

Lotus 1-2-3 Release 2.3

Macintosh Software

Microsoft Word for the Macintosh

Microsoft Word for the PC

Norton Utilities 5

Norton Utilities 6

PageMaker 4.0 for the Macintosh

Paradox 3.5

PC Tools Deluxe 6

Quattro Pro 3

Windows 3.0

WordPerfect 5

WordPerfect 5.1

Computer users are not all alike.
Neither are SYBEX books.

We know our customers have a variety of needs. They've told us so. And because we've listened, we've developed several distinct types of books to meet the needs of each of our customers. What are you looking for in computer help?

If you're looking for the basics, try the **ABC's** series, or for a more visual approach, select **Teach Yourself.**

Mastering and **Understanding** titles offer you a step-by-step introduction, plus an in-depth examination of intermediate-level features, to use as you progress.

Our **Up & Running** series is designed for computer-literate consumers who want a no-nonsense overview of new programs. Just 20 basic lessons, and you're on your way.

SYBEX **Encyclopedias** and **Desktop References** provide a *comprehensive reference* and explanation of all of the commands, features, and functions of the subject software.

Sometimes a subject requires a special treatment that our standard series doesn't provide. So you'll find we have titles like **Advanced Techniques, Handbooks, Tips & Tricks,** and others that are specifically tailored to satisfy a unique need.

You'll find SYBEX publishes a variety of books on every popular software package. Looking for computer help? Help Yourself to SYBEX.

For a complete catalog of our publications:

SYBEX, Inc.
2021 Challenger Drive, Alameda, CA 94501
Tel: (510) 523-8233/(800) 227-2346 Telex: 336311
Fax: (510) 523-2373

SYBEX is committed to using natural resources wisely to preserve and improve our environment. This is why we have been printing the text of books like this one on recycled paper since 1982.

This year our use of recycled paper will result in the saving of more than 15,300 trees. We will lower air pollution effluents by 54,000 pounds, save 6,300,000 gallons of water, and reduce landfill by 2,700 cubic yards.

In choosing a SYBEX book you are not only making a choice for the best in skills and information, you are also choosing to enhance the quality of life for all of us.

Norton Desktop™ for Windows™ Instant Reference

Sharon Crawford and Charlie Russel

San Francisco • Paris • Düsseldorf • Soest

Acquisitions Editor: Dianne King
Developmental Editor: James A. Compton
Editor: Kayla Sussell
Technical Editor: Sheila Dienes
Word Processors: Ann Dunn, Susan Trybull
Series Designer: Ingrid Owen
Production Artist: Lucie Živny
Screen Graphics: Cuong Le
Desktop Publishing Specialist: M.D. Barrera
Proofreader/Production Assistant: Elizabeth G. Chuan
Indexer: Kathleen Garcia

Cover Designer: Archer Designs

Acknowledgments

Thanks are due to

- The hardworking production staff at Sybex: especially word processors Ann Dunn and Susan Trybull, desktop publishing specialist M.D. Barrera, proofreader/production assistant, Elizabeth G. Chuan, and Cuong Le who produced the screen graphics

- Our wonderful and meticulous technical editor, Sheila Dienes

- Our diligent and creative editor, Kayla Sussell

- Developmental editor Jim Compton, whose thoughtful advice was invaluable

- Our painstaking production artist, Lucie Živny

- Dianne King for her generous and enthusiastic support through trying times

- Michael Gross for providing encouragement at the beginning and amusement throughout, and

- friends and colleagues who tolerated our wailing and gnashing of teeth during the whole process.

Any errors are our responsibility and any credit must be shared with all of the above.

Table of Contents

Part Three
RUNNING QUICK ACCESS

Part Four
TOOLS AND UTILITIES

Part Five
NORTON BACKUP

Part Six
CONFIGURING THE DESKTOP

Appendix A

INSTALLATION
149

Appendix B

THE NORTON WINDOWS BATCH LANGUAGE
153

Appendix C

THE EMERGENCY DISKETTE PROGRAMS
179

Index

Introduction

The Norton Desktop for Windows offers quick and elegant solutions to many of the problems that can plague users of Windows 3.0. In addition to Windows versions of the familiar Norton disk utilities, the new package includes features designed to bypass the File Manager and Program Manager, making Windows even easier to use.

Using the Drive Windows, you can move, copy, print, or even back up files with just a few mouse clicks. Quick Access allows you to set up groups and subgroups in ways that are completely independent of your DOS menu structure. These tools have no equivalent in Windows. The Norton Desktop for Windows package offers dozens of ways to configure your system to fit your specific working needs, and you can choose to use all of these or just a few. This book presents them all clearly and simply.

Instant Reference books are intended to provide quick access to all the functions of a program. In the case of Norton Desktop for Windows, so many options are available that it may take you a while to become familiar with them. The aim of this book is to give you, in brief form, the essential information that you will need to answer any questions that may come up while you are using the program. You need not be an experienced user of either Norton Desktop or Windows. Explanations for all of the terms used can be found in Part I. If you have not yet installed Norton Desktop for Windows, see Appendix A for a guide to installation.

HOW THIS BOOK IS ORGANIZED

Part One, "An Overview of the Norton Desktop for Windows," includes descriptions of the main features of the package and definitions and descriptions of all the terms used in this book. Note that both Windows and Norton Desktop for Windows use the same names for the various buttons, boxes, and other parts of the interface.

Part Two, "Managing Files," covers the File Management functions, including the Drive Windows, the highly useful substitute for the File Manager in Windows. This is where you will find the commands for copying, moving, deleting, and otherwise manipulating files.

Part Three, "Running Quick Access," covers all of the functions in Quick Access. This module offers you new ways for organizing your files and applications into groups and subgroups that are tailored to fit your specific needs. Quick Access can be run either as a stand-alone program or as a seamless part of the Norton Desktop for Windows environment.

Part Four, "Tools and Utilities," includes the following:

- **Batch Builder**: This utility is a notepad for building and editing Windows batch files.

- **Calculator**: This utility includes a scientific calculator and a ten-key calculator with a tape.

- **Disk Doctor**: This utility program checks the computer for both existing and potential problems.

- **Icon Editor**: This tool allows you to modify program and system icons and to design your own icons.

- **KeyFinder**: This utility locates special character codes for inclusion in Windows applications.

- **Scheduler**: This program runs other programs and displays message reminders.

- **Shredder**: This tool will remove files from your system permanently.

- **Sleeper**: This is a screen saver program with optional password protection.

- **SuperFind**: This program performs file and text searches.

- **System Info**: This tool provides detailed information on all aspects of your computer's operation.

- **UnErase/SmartErase**: This tool restores accidentally deleted files.

Part Five, "Norton Backup," is devoted to the operations of the Norton Backup program. This program can help you to safeguard your files through the use of selective or general backups.

Part Six, "Configuring the Desktop," covers the many configuration options for the desktop. Here you will find the means to change how the Norton Desktop looks and behaves.

At the end of the book there are three Appendices. Appendix A covers the installation of the Norton Desktop for Windows, Appendix B describes the commands available in the Batch Language, and Appendix C discusses the use of the Emergency Diskette programs.

Part One

An Overview of the Norton Desktop for Windows

The Norton Desktop for Windows package can organize and facilitate every aspect of your work inside Windows 3.0. The new features that have been designed to replace the inconvenient File Manager and the inflexible Program Manager change the way your desktop looks and the ease with which it operates. The package includes many new tools and accessories as well as the means to adjust virtually every aspect of your computer's look, feel, and operation within the Windows environment.

For the most part, this book assumes that you are running Norton Desktop for Windows as your Windows shell and that you have enabled Quick Access. (See Appendix A for information on installation options.) If you are not using Norton Desktop as a shell, you will need to open the Norton Desktop group and then select the Norton Desktop icon to reach the menus and functions that are described.

If you intend to use only the tools and utilities, you can decline to run the Norton Desktop as your shell and just select specific tool icons from the Norton Desktop group as you need them for particular tasks.

Most functions in Norton Desktop for Windows, as in Windows, can be activated either from the keyboard or by using a mouse. Instructions in this book will usually indicate to "select" or to "click on" a given choice. This can be done with the mouse or by keystrokes to move the cursor.

USING THE KEYBOARD

Menus can be pulled down by pressing the Alt key and the letter that is underlined in the menu name. When the menu is visible, you make your selection by keying in the letter that is underlined in the name.

In a dialog box, the cursor appears as a dotted line outlining the choice. The cursor also appears as a vertical line in a text box within a dialog box. To turn a selection on or off, press the space bar while the cursor outlines that choice. When the cursor is on a button, press ↵ to choose that option. Inside a dialog box, the cursor can be moved using the ↑, ↓, ←, or → keys as well as the Tab key.

USING A MOUSE

To click on an item, first position the mouse pointer over that item. Then press the left mouse button once and release. Double-clicking means that you position the pointer over the item and press the button twice in rapid succession.

To drag an item, click on it and hold the mouse button down. When you move the mouse, you will see the item pulled along the screen. When you reach the location where you want to place the item, release the mouse button.

To select an item from a menu, click on the menu name. While holding the mouse button down, move the mouse until the item you want becomes highlighted, then release the button. You can also select an item from a menu by clicking once on the menu name, and once on the menu item.

To select multiple items from a list, such as a directory of files, you can use one of the following two methods:

Shift-click   To select contiguous items on a list, hold the **Shift** key down and click on the first item you want. Keep the Shift key depressed and move to the last item and click on it. The first, last, and all items between will be highlighted.

Control-click   To select noncontiguous items on a list, hold down the **Ctrl** key while clicking on the items you want.

MENUS

In the Norton Desktop there is a menu bar with the names of the menus at the top of the screen. Click on the name of the menu, and the listing will appear below it. By default, the program opens with the short version of the menus. To see the full listing you must select Full Menus from the Configuration menu.

Menu names include other indications as to their functions. For example, an ellipsis (…) following a menu name signifies that choosing that item will open a dialog box where other choices are made. A solid triangle (▶) after an item means that a submenu will appear when that item is highlighted.

Some menu items, such as the first three items under the View menu, are toggles. (A *toggled* item is alternately turned off and on each time you select it.) When you select one of these, a check mark will appear indicating that the function is toggled on. When you click on the item again, the check mark will disappear and the function will be toggled off.

Note that several choices in the Window menu are available only when a group window is open. Likewise, dimmed-out functions are not available for use. For example, the Net Drive functions in the Disk menu are dimmed-out unless you are on a network.

BOXES AND BUTTONS

Virtually everything you do in Norton Desktop for Windows must be done by means of various boxes and buttons. It may seem that there are a great many names for similar functions, but you should familiarize yourself with these names because the names themselves signify how the box or button can be used. All boxes are in dialog boxes; when you choose a menu item, a dialog box opens.

Browse Box   When you select a browse button, a browse box will open. It usually includes file, directory, and drive icons so that you can locate files whose exact name or location you may not remember. When you find the file and select it, and then click on **OK**, the filename will be returned to the original dialog box.

Check Box   A square box next to an item is a check box that can be turned on or off. To select that item, click on the **square box**. An X will appear to indicate that the item is toggled on. To turn the choice off, select the **square box** again and the X will disappear.

Speed Search Box   A speed search box is the quickest way to find a file or directory in a Tree Pane or File Pane. When you start typing the name of the file or directory, the speed search box appears below the active pane and the cursor bar moves to highlight the first file or directory that matches the letters typed. When the cursor bar has moved to the file or directory you want, press ↵ to select it.

Tri-State Box   A tri-state box is just like a check box except that it has three settings. If there is an X in the box, the option is turned on. If the setting is blank, the option is turned off. If the box is a solid gray, the program will disregard whether the option is on or off.

Text Box   A text box appears as a blank box into which you key in text or numbers. Click anywhere in the text box and a blinking vertical line representing your cursor will appear at the left side of the box. Begin keying in text where the cursor indicates. To make a change in your text, press the **Backspace** key, or click and drag the mouse across the part of the text that you want to change and highlight it. Then press the **Delete** key.

Insert mode is the default, so you can also press the **right** or **left arrow** keys and insert (or delete) text. You can also use the mouse to move the cursor to a different location in a text box that has text in it.

Drop Down Box   A drop down box appears as a text box with a choice already indicated inside it and a prompt button on the right side of the box. Click on the **prompt button** and the box will open downward and reveal other choices that can be selected.

Combination Box   A combination box looks and acts like a drop down box except that in addition to the choices provided, you can also key in your own choice.

Dialog Box   A dialog box is a small window that allows you to select the options available for the program or function chosen. The term dialog box is often used in Windows and refers to any box in which user choices are available. Dialog boxes always appear when you choose any menu command that contains an ellipsis (…).

Control Box   The control box is at the upper left-hand corner of the main Norton Desktop window and all other windows and dialog boxes. It is a gray box with a slotlike mark. To see the Control box menu, click on the control box.

Command Button   When selected, a command button causes the program to execute an action. Command buttons include OK, Cancel, Select, Browse, and so forth. They are rectangularly shaped and when they are selected, they appear to depress.

Prompt Button   A prompt button is located on the right side of a drop down or combination box. It has a downward pointing arrow on it to indicate that when it is activated, it will make more choices available.

Radio Button   Radio buttons function just like the selection buttons on a radio. Only one can be on at a time. To select one is to deselect any other. Usually, a radio button is round and when it is toggled on, its center darkens.

Minimize/Maximize Buttons   At the upper right-hand corner of the Norton Desktop there are many program screens. In addition, there are some buttons with either up or down arrows and some buttons with both up and down arrows. A button showing both up and down arrows indicates that the window is at its maximum size; clicking on that button will reduce the window to its normal operating size. To minimize the size of the window, select a button with a **downward pointing arrow**. Note that a program that has been minimized remains open. To maximize the size of the window, select a button with an **upward pointing arrow**.

Help Button   A help button is available in most windows and dialog boxes. When you select this button, an information screen will appear based on the program or function you are using. These help screens operate like the Windows help screens. Consult your Windows documentation for more information on using the help system.

BARS

Bars appear on dialog boxes and other windows. The title bar, menu bar, and scroll bars provide information on the window's function and contents.

Title Bar   The title bar appears at the top of every window and box. The name of the program or dialog box is written there. To move a window, click on the title bar and drag the window to the location you choose.

Menu Bar   The menu bar is just below the title bar. Only the titles of available menus appear on the menu bar. When you select a menu name, a list appears with any currently unavailable menus dimmed.

Scroll Bar   Whenever the information in a window will not fit into the available space, the window will have a scroll bar on its right edge. To move up or down in the window, click on the **up** or **down arrow**. To move more rapidly, click and drag the slider box in the scroll bar.

Some windows will also have horizontal scroll bars that work in the same manner, except that they move from side to side.

ICONS

An icon is a miniature, graphic representation of a program, a tool, a file, or a group. When a program is "iconized" it remains open on the desktop without taking up desk space. Simply click on the **minimize button** and programs can continue to run while you are doing something else.

When you are ready to return to the iconized program, you can click it open again without having to search through a directory or key in instructions.

Drive Icons   When Norton Desktop opens, you will see icons that represent your computer drives on the left side of the screen as shown in Figure I-1. The top two icons, looking like small diskette drives, represent your floppy A: and B: disk drives. Below these, there will be an icon for each of your hard drives. If you have a RAM or network drive, a special icon for that drive will also appear. These icons can be selected to open Drive Windows.

Program Icons   When Norton Desktop for Windows starts, several icons representing the program tools appear on the right side of the screen. Icons representing programs also appear in all the group windows. Icons can be dragged from the group windows to

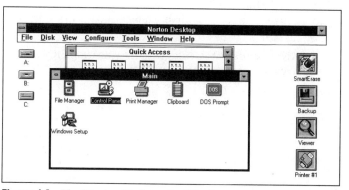

Figure I.1: The Norton Desktop for Windows initial screen

the desktop where they will remain until selected and closed. Programs can be opened by double-clicking on the program icon.

Group Icons   Group icons represent an entire group of applications. There are icons in the Quick Access window that each represent a group of programs.

WILDCARDS

Norton Desktop for Windows recognizes the following wildcard characters:

?   Represents a single character at the corresponding position.

*   Represents all the remaining characters in the field.

¦   Represents one or zero characters.

Note that the entries in this book specify those cases where wildcards cannot be used.

• EXAMPLES

BUDGET.PR?   Represents all files with the name BUDGET where the extension begins with the letters PR but any character can be in the third position.

BUDGET.*   Represents all files with the name BUDGET but any characters can be used in the extension.

¦¦.PRN   Represents all files with the extension PRN that also have two or fewer characters in their names.

Part Two

Managing Files

ASSOCIATE A FILE EXTENSION WITH A PROGRAM

When you associate a filename extension with an application, you can then select any file with that extension and the associated program will open automatically. Norton Desktop for Windows automates Windows association of file extensions with programs. This makes it easy to add, change, or delete associations through the use of dialog boxes, as well as providing the ability to include startup commands.

To Add an Association

1. Select **Associate** from the File menu.

2. Select **Add** to bring up the Add Extension dialog box.

3. Key in the application program's full path name (including extension) or .PIF filename in the Program Name box. You can also use the Browse button to find the program's filename and path.

4. In the extension box, key in the extension to associate with this program. Do *not* include the period (.) in the extension. If you use the Browse button, you can double-click on the filename, and the path and filename will appear in the Add Extension Program text box.

5. The Optional Command Line box will show the extension, preceded by a caret (^). This will automatically expand to the full program name plus the filename when the associated file is opened from anywhere in Norton Desktop for Windows.

6. Click on **OK**. This returns you to the Associate dialog box. To confirm the addition, click on **OK** again.

• EXAMPLE

Quattro Pro will read and write Quattro Pro files and Lotus 1-2-3 files. The default file extension for Quattro Pro files is .WQ1 and for Lotus 1-2-3 worksheets it is .WK1. To associate .WQ1 and .WK1 files with Quattro Pro so that selecting a file with either extension will start Quattro Pro automatically, select **Associate** from the File menu, click on the **Add button** and key in **QP.PIF** in the Program Name box. Then key in **WQ1** in the extension box. Click on **OK** and select **Add** again, and using **WK1** this time, repeat the steps.

When you are finished adding the file extensions to Quattro Pro, you must click on **OK** again to confirm the additions or **Cancel** to return to the original condition.

To Change an Association

1. Select **Associate** from the File menu.
2. From the List box select the extension you wish to change.
3. Select **Edit** to bring up the Edit Extension dialog box.
4. Key in the **new file extension** in place of the old one.
5. Select **OK**. This returns you to the Associate dialog box. To confirm that your change has been made, select **OK** again.

To Delete an Association

1. Select **Associate** from the File menu.
2. From the List box, select the **extension** to delete.
3. Select **Delete**. The highlighted association will be deleted immediately.
4. Select **OK** to confirm the deletion, or **Cancel** to abandon the change.

To Specify a Custom Startup Command

1. Select **Associate** from the File menu.

2. Select **Add** to add a new association, or highlight an existing extension and then select **Edit**.

3. If you are adding a new association, fill in the Program and Extension text boxes.

4. Press **Alt+O** or click on the **Optional Command Line** box, and key in the command line parameters to pass to the program when the program is run.

5. Select OK to confirm the command line parameters. Then select OK again in the Associate dialog box to confirm all changes to the file association or Cancel to abandon them.

● EXAMPLE

One useful parameter that can be passed to Quattro Pro is **/d123.rf** which instructs the program to open with Lotus-like menus. To change the file association you just created so that it will open 1-2-3 files in Quattro Pro automatically with such Lotus-like menus, highlight **WK1** in the Associations box and click on the **Edit** button. In the Optional Command Line box add **/d123.rf** in front of the ^.**WK1**. (Note that there must be one space between /d123.rf and ^.WK1.) Click on **OK** twice. Now, when you open a .WK1 file, it will open Quattro Pro automatically, but it will use the Lotus-like menu instead of the Quattro Pro default menu.

● NOTES Norton Desktop For Windows does not allow wildcards in associated extensions. You must explicitly specify each extension that you wish to associate with a given program.

A particular extension can be associated only with a single program, but any program can have as many extensions associated with it as needed.

See Also Launch Functions

ATTRIBUTES

Files can have four possible attributes—Hidden, System, Read Only, and Archive. Usually, hidden files are not visible, but they can be seen in Norton Desktop for Windows if desired. System files are also hidden from normal view. DOS uses the system attribute to designate files that it employs during the initial boot sequence. Read Only files can be viewed with the Viewer or copied, but they cannot be edited, changed, or deleted. The Archive attribute indicates whether a file has been backed up since the last time it was modified.

To Change File Attributes

1. Open a Drive Window.

2. Highlight the file or files you want to change.

3. Select **Properties** from the File menu.

4. For more than one file, select from the tri-state options in the Attributes box. For only one file, toggle the Attribute options on or off.

5. Select **OK** to confirm the operation, or **Cancel** to abandon the change.

● EXAMPLE

If you want to make sure that a file is designated Read Only, change the Read Only attribute box to an X. If you want to ensure that the file is not marked Read Only, click on the Read Only attribute box until it is blank. If the file you have highlighted does not have a grayed Read Only status (or other attribute), you cannot make it gray.

● **NOTE**   If no file is highlighted, but a Group window is active, the Group Properties dialog box will be opened, as shown in Figure II.1. This dialog box allows you to modify group properties.

Figure II.1: The Group Properties dialog box

COPY A FILE

The Copy command lets you copy a single file or whole subdirectories. It can be used from the desktop, or when in the Drive Windows. The Copy command can be activated from the File drop down menu by pressing **F8**, or from the Button bar when in the Drive Windows. You can also click on the file or subdirectory icons and drag them to the target location.

To Copy a File or Files

1.   Open a Drive Window.

2.   Highlight the file or files that you want to copy. If you want to copy a subdirectory or subdirectories, highlight them.

3.   Select **Copy** from the File menu, press **F8**, click on the **Copy** button on the Button bar, or drag the file to another open Drive Window.

4.   Unless you dragged the file to another open Drive Window, the Copy dialog box opens with a Destination combination box. Key in the destination, select from the list of recent destinations, or click on **Select** to open an enhanced Copy dialog box and then choose the destination. This enhanced box also shows the amount of disk space used, and the amount of free disk space remaining.

5.   Select **OK** to begin the copy operation, or **Cancel** to abandon it.

● **NOTES**   To copy subdirectories from the source directory, check the **Include Subdirectories** box in the Copy dialog box.

If you activate a group instead of a file, the Copy program dialog box opens and you can copy objects in one group to another group. To copy an object from one Group window to another, click on the **item** while pressing **Ctrl**. Keep the Ctrl key depressed while dragging the icon to its destination. To copy a Group window, drag the group icon into another Group window.

● **SHORTCUT**   Drag one or more file icons to the destination directory in the directory tree on the left side of the Drive Window, or drag the icon (or icons) to a directory in another Drive Window.

See Also   Drive Windows

DELETE A FILE

The File Delete command allows you to delete a single file, multiple files, or entire subdirectories.

To Delete a File or Files

1.   Open a Drive Window.

2.   Highlight the file(s) or subdirectory you wish to delete.

3.   Select **Delete** from the File menu and press the **Delete** button on the Button bar, or press the **Del** key on your keyboard.

4.   If you select OK, a Warning window appears with these choices: Yes; Yes to All; No; Cancel. You must choose one. This happens unless you toggle off **Delete** on the Configure Confirmation window.

● **SHORTCUT**   Click on the file or subdirectory in a Drive Window and drag it to the **SmartErase** or **Shredder** icon on the desktop.

● **NOTE**   If no group or Drive Window is open on the desktop, select **Delete** from the File menu.

See Also   Drive Windows, Shredder (Part IV), SmartErase (Part IV)

DRIVE WINDOWS

The Drive Windows are at the heart of the Norton Desktop for Windows. They replace the Windows File Manager by allowing you to copy, move, delete, view, and find files easily with a click or two of a button. By default, the Drive Window buttons appear on the left side of the desktop, and include all available drives including networked drives; but, like most things in Norton Desktop for Windows, this is configurable.

To Configure the Drive Icons

1. Select **Drive Icons** from the Configure menu.

2. Use the mouse to highlight the individual drive icons.

3. If you also want to specify, **All Hard Disks, All Network Drives**, or **All Floppy Drives**, click on the appropriate check boxes in Drive Types.

4. To display the drive icons, click on the **check box** and select a **radio button** to choose the display location.

5. Select **OK** to confirm the choices, or **Cancel** to return to the previous configuration.

To Open a Drive Window

To open a Drive Window, double-click on the **drive icon** on the Desktop, or select **Open Drive Window** from the Window menu. You can have more than one Drive Window for the same drive open at the same time, and windows for more than one drive can be open as well. Figure II.2 illustrates the component parts of a Drive Window.

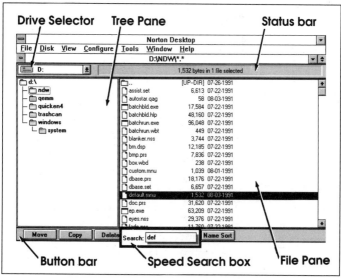

Figure II.2: The parts of a Drive Window

THE PARTS OF A DRIVE WINDOW

The various parts of the Drive Window work together to make it easy to do most file operations with a click or two. The components of the Drive Window are listed below.

The **Status Bar** displays information about the drive, directory, or file(s) selected.

The **Drive Selector** is a combination box. It allows you to change drives without opening up another Drive Window. To change drives, highlight this box and key in the letter of the drive, or click on the drop down box **prompt button** and select the **drive**.

The **Button Bar** has up to six buttons that can be configured to whatever file functions are the most commonly used. By default, these are Move, Copy, Delete, View Pane, Type Sort, and Name Sort. To modify these settings, see *Button Bar* in Part VI, "Configuring the Desktop."

The **Copy**, **Move**, and **Delete** buttons all work in a similar manner. To copy a file, highlight the file or files in the File Pane, and then click on the **Copy button**. This opens up the Copy dialog box. Key in the destination to the Destination combination box, or select the **prompt button** to pull down a list of recent destinations. Alternatively, you can pick the **Select button** to open an enhanced dialog box. When the Destination box is correct, select **OK** to confirm the copy, or **Cancel** to abandon the change.

The **Type Sort** button toggles the display to show the files sorted by extension.

The **View Pane** button is a toggle. Click on it to open the View Pane. Click on it again to close the View Pane. The View Pane should not be confused with the Viewer, which also allows you to view files, but is more versatile.

The **Name Sort** button toggles the display to show the files sorted by filename.

The **Panes** make up the main body of the Drive Window. They display the selected drive's tree structure, a file list, and, optionally, with View Pane toggled on, the contents of the currently selected file.

The **Speed Search Box** is the quickest way to find a file or directory in either the Tree Pane or the File Pane. Note that you must start keying in characters for the Speed Search box to appear. When you begin keying in the name of the file or directory, the Speed Search box appears below the appropriate pane and the cursor bar moves to highlight the first file or directory that matches the keyed-in letters. When the cursor bar has moved to the file or directory you want, press **Enter** to select it.

If the Tree Pane is active, the Speed Search box works in the Tree Pane. If the File Pane is active, the Speed Search box works there. Press the **Tab** key to cycle the pane highlighter through the drive selecter, Tree Pane, File Pane, and Button bar.

To Refresh the Drive Windows

The display of files and directories in the Drive Windows does not always update automatically as moves, deletions, and so forth, are made. To update the display, select **Refresh** from the View menu, or press **F5**.

To Configure the Panes

From the View menu, select from the following:

- **Tree Pane** to toggle the Tree Pane on and off.
- **File Pane** to toggle the File Pane on and off.
- **View Pane** to toggle the View Pane on and off.
- **Show Entire Drive** to replace the Tree and File Panes with a pane showing all the files on the drive and their locations.

To Filter the File Display in the File Pane

1. Select **Filter** from the View menu to bring up the Filter dialog box.

2. From the list in the File Type box, select the **file types** to display:

   - Select **All Files** to show all the files.

- Select **Programs** to show all executable programs (.COM, .EXE, .BAT, .PIF).
- Select **Documents** to show all document files (.DOC, .WRI, .TXT).
- Select **Custom** to define a custom filter.

3. If you chose Custom, fill in the combination box with the file specification(s) that you want displayed, or choose from a list of recent selections. (Note that Custom can be used with wildcards in the file specifications.)

4. From the Attributes box, choose which files to display by attribute.

5. Select **OK** to confirm the choices, or **Cancel** to return to the previous configuration.

• EXAMPLES

- Toggle the **Hidden** attribute to blank to exclude hidden files.
- Toggle the **Archive** attribute to gray to see files regardless of whether they have been backed up or not.
- Choose **Custom**, then key in ~*.W?? to see all Lotus and Quattro Pro spreadsheet files.
- Choose **Custom**, then key in ~*.XLS *.W?? to see all spreadsheet files, including Excel files.

To Change the File Pane Detail

1. Select **File Details** from the View menu to bring up the File Details dialog box.

2. Select the File **options** that you want to see displayed in the File Pane. Items marked with an X will show in the pane. The sample line shows how the files will appear.

3. Select **OK** to confirm the choices, or **Cancel** to return to the previous configuration.

● OPTIONS

Icon   Toggle the display of file icons. An icon for a text file resembles a page with lines of writing on it. Executable files, such as programs and batch files, have icons that resemble on-screen windows. All other files have icons that look like a blank page of paper.

Date   Toggles the inclusion of the file creation date in the display.

Attributes   Toggles whether the file display includes the file attributes (Hidden, System, Read Only, or Archive).

Size   Toggles the inclusion of the file size in the display.

Time   Toggles whether the file creation time is included in the display.

Directory   Toggles the display of the file's directory. (Active only in **Show Entire Drive** mode.)

To Change the Sort Order in the File Pane

1.   Select **Sort By** from the View menu.

2.   Use the mouse to highlight the file characteristic by which to sort, or select ascending or descending sort order. The display will be updated immediately.

● OPTIONS

Name   Sorts alphabetically by filename.

Type   Sorts alphabetically by file extension.

Size   Sorts by file size.

Date   Sorts by file creation date and time.

Unsorted   Displays files in DOS order.

Ascending   Displays files in alphabetical order, smallest to largest, or most recent to oldest.

Descending   Displays files in reverse alphabetical order, largest to smallest, or oldest to most recent.

• **NOTES**   By default, the primary sort order is by filename. If type, size, or date is chosen as the primary sort, then the secondary sort is by name. The default sort is performed in ascending order (A before Z, 1980 before 1991, small before large) unless descending order is checked.

EDIT A FILE

Files can be edited using either the default Editor, Windows Notepad, or an editor of your choice. To select another editor see "Editor" in Part VI, "Configuring the Desktop."

To Edit a File

1.   Select **Edit** from the File menu.

   • If no Drive Window was open, the Edit dialog box will open. In the Edit text box, key in the **name**, including the **path**, of the file you want to edit. Click on **OK**.

   • If a Drive Window is open and a file is highlighted, a Notepad window opens and displays the highlighted file.

   • If a Drive Window is open and no file is highlighted, a blank Notepad window opens. Select **Open** from the File menu and key in the **name** of the file to be edited. Click on **OK**.

2.   Edit the file. Select **Save** from the File menu to save your changes. Choose **Exit** from the File menu to leave Notepad.

• **NOTES**   Wildcards are not allowed in selecting a filename, and multiple files may not be selected to edit.

LAUNCH FUNCTIONS

The Launch Manager and Launch List are located in all the Control
Box menus generated inside Norton Desktop for Windows. Using
Launch, you can open a file and its associated application from virtually anywhere in Norton Desktop for Windows. When you
launch an application or script, it executes. When you open a document file, its associated application executes and the file opens. If
the file is not associated with an application, the result will be an
error message.

To Configure the Launch Manager

1. Select **Launch Manager** from any Control Box menu.

2. To add a menu item, click on **Add**. In the Text box, key in
the name of the item as you want it to appear on the
Launch List. If you want to add an Alt+key accelerator to
this command, place an ampersand just before the
accelerator's letter.

3. In the Command Line box, key in the path for the item.

4. To associate a shortcut key combination with the item, key
in a two-key combination of Shift, Alt, or Ctrl and any
second key. If you want the menu listing to show the
shortcut key, click on the **check box**. Select **OK** twice to
confirm the addition.

• OPTIONS

Edit   Use the mouse to highlight a menu item and select **Edit**
to modify any item on the menu.

Delete   Highlight the item and then click on **Delete** to
remove the item from the Launch List.

Move Up/Move Down   Highlight a menu item and then
click on **Move Up** or **Move Down** to change an item's position
on the Launch List.

24 Managing Files

● **NOTE**   By default, Norton Desktop for Windows starts the Launch Manager with the following programs already listed:

- Format diskette
- Copy diskette
- SuperFind
- Tape calculator
- Scheduler
- Control Panel (from Windows)
- KeyFinder
- Sleeper

To Launch a File from the Launch Manager

1. Pull down the Control Box menu anywhere in Norton Desktop for Windows.

2. Highlight Launch List and a list of launchable programs/documents will drop down as shown in Figure II.3. Select the desired item and the application will execute.

To Launch a File from a File Pane

1. Select **Open Drive Window** from the Window menu or double-click on the appropriate drive icon.

2. Double-click on the filename in the Drive Window.

To Launch a File from a Group Window

- Double-click on the selected icon in its Group Window.

To Launch a File from a File Icon

1. Open the appropriate Drive Window and select the file from the file list.

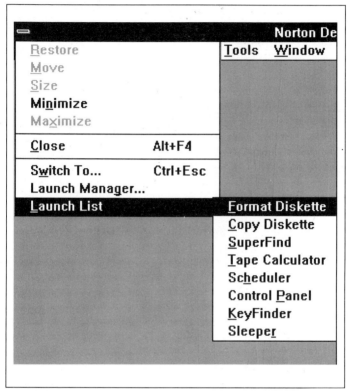

Figure II.3: The Launch List

2.   Drag the file's icon to the name of the application on the
list. This name must have an .EXE or .COM extension. The
application will execute and the file will open.

Note that before the application executes, a Warning message appears:

**Are you sure you want to start (application) using
(filename) as the initial file?**

● **NOTE**   This procedure can also be used to open files not associated
with an application. In addition, it will work with a file that has an extension associated with a different application than the one you want to

use. However, if you drag the file to an application icon on the desktop, the file will not open, and the file icon will remain on the desktop until you close it.

To Launch a File from the Command Line

1. Select **Run** from the File menu.

2. If the file is associated with an application, key in the file **name** and **extension** only. If the file does not have an association with an application, key in the **full pathname**.

● **OPTIONS**

Previous launches   Select the **prompt box** next to the Run Window's Command Line text box and a list will appear of the last ten applications launched.

Normal   Applications will launch in their normal configuration.

Minimized   When selected, an application will shrink to icon size automatically as soon as it is launched.

Maximized   Causes launched files to appear full screen on your desktop.

Browse   Allows you to search through all drives and directories to select applications and files.

See Also   Associate a File Extension with a Program, Drive Windows

MAKE A DIRECTORY

When directories become too large, you can make a new subdirectory to keep track of your files.

To Make a New Directory

1. Choose **Make Directory...** from the File menu.

2. A dialog box opens and you can key in the **name**, including the path, of the directory you wish to create in the New Directory text box. Click on the **Select** button to choose another drive or directory to identify the path you want.

3. Select the **OK** button to confirm your choice.

MOVE A FILE

To move a file rather than copy it, follow the steps below.

To Move a File

1. Open a Drive Window.

2. Highlight the file(s) or subdirectory you wish to move.

3. Select **Move** from the File menu, select the **Move** button on the Button bar, or press **F7**. In the To text box, key in the **file destination**, including the path.

4. Click on the **OK** button when finished.

• NOTES

To choose a destination, click on the **Select** button to see a directory tree of the current drive, including a display of available space. Click on the **directory name** of the target location, and then click on **OK**. Other drives can be selected from the Destination drop-down box.

If a group is highlighted instead of a file or subdirectory, the Move Group dialog box is opened, as shown in Figure II.4.

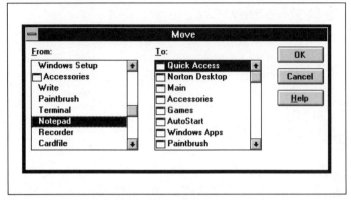

Figure II.4: A Move Group dialog box

OPEN A FILE

A file with an extension that is associated with a program or a file with an .EXE, .BAT, .COM, or .PIF extension can be opened by clicking on the file in a **Drive Window** and then pressing the **Enter** key.

See Also   Associate a File Extension with a Program

PRINT FILES

To Print a File

1. Select **Print** from the File menu.

2. Key in the **name** of the file to be printed in the Print text box.

3. Select **OK**.

Click on the **Browse** button to see a list of files sorted by directory within the current drive. Use the mouse to change drives and directories and to select a filename.

● **SHORTCUT**   Drag the file's icon from an open Drive Window to the Printer Icon on the desktop.

● **NOTES**   If you drag the file to the Printer tool icon on the desktop, Norton Desktop for Windows checks to see if the file has an extension associated with an application in the associations list. If no association exists, Norton Desktop for Windows will ask if you want to print the file unformatted. If you select Yes, the file will print. The results, however, may be incomplete or garbled.

If an association exists, the application will open and the name of the document file will be passed to the application. Norton Desktop for Windows will then send the keystrokes Alt-P, F to the application. This assumes that the application has a menu command named File Print. Norton Desktop for Windows then minimizes the application and switches back to the desktop. If these steps do not work—and they will not for many non-Windows applications—you will need to take the following steps in "To Set Up a Print Keystroke Sequence."

To Set Up a Print Keystroke Sequence

1.   Using Notepad or another text editor, open the existing NDW.INI file.

2.   Add a section with the heading

   (Print Start)

3.   Under the heading, add a line in the form

   filename.exe=start key sequence

   where filename is the name of the program and start key sequence describes the keystrokes that will print the current file.

4.   Add a section called:

[**Print Stop**]

5.   Under that, add a line in the form:

filename.exe=stop key sequence

where *filename* is the name of the program and stop key sequence describes the keystrokes that will close and exit the application.

6.   Save the changes to NDW.INI and restart Norton Desktop for Windows.

The start and stop key sequence can contain Alt and Ctrl keys as well as function keys using the following codes:

Key	Code
Alt+key	!key
Ctrl+key	^key
Enter	{Enter} or ~
F1 through F16	{F1} through {F16}

To Print Associated Files Directly

1.   Using a text editor, open the file NDW.INI. Add a section named:

(Print Start)

2.   In that section, add a line:

filename.exe=

where *filename* is the name of the program associated with the file you want to print. Leave the right side of the equal sign blank.

3.   Save the changes to NDW.INI and restart Norton Desktop for Windows.

To Change Printers or Printer Settings

1. Select **Print** from the File Menu. To change the printer, open the Printer drop down box and select another printer. In the Print dialog box, select **Setup**.

2. The first dialog box gives information on your current printer.

3. The Setup options are the same as the Windows printer settings. Changes made here affect how the printer works with all Windows applications.

See Also   Drive Windows

RENAME FILES OR SUBDIRECTORIES

A single file or a subdirectory can be renamed quickly. Simply enter the name or search for it as described below.

To Rename a File or Subdirectory

1. Open a Drive Window.

2. Highlight the file or subdirectory you want to rename.

3. Select **Rename** from the File menu.

4. Key in the **new path** and **name** in the To text box. Select **OK**.

● **NOTE**   For help in finding the file to be renamed, select the **Browse** button for a drive and directory tree. Use the mouse to scan the choices and click on the **file**, then select **OK** to confirm the selection.

VIEW FILES

The Viewer will display a file according to the file's extension. For example, .DOC indicates a file written in Microsoft Word. If the file lacks an extension, the Viewer will display the file according to the default setting. The available default settings are the following:

- Compressed Archives
- CompuServe GIF
- dBase
- Documents and Text
- Hex Dump
- Lotus 1-2-3
- Microsoft Excel
- Paintbrush (PCX)
- Programs
- TIFF (Grayscale and Color)
- Windows Bitmaps
- Windows Icons
- WordPerfect Image Graphics

If you have a TIFF graphics image file, for example, without an extension or with an extension that does not identify it as a TIFF file, you will not be able to view the file unless the Viewer's default setting is TIFF (Grayscale and Color).

To View a File

1. Double-click on the **Viewer** desktop icon or the **File Viewer** icon in the Norton Desktop Group Window. The Norton Viewer window will pop up on your desktop.

2. Select **Open** from the File menu. Choose the file you want
to view from the Browse box. Click on **OK**. The file will appear in its own window inside the Viewer window. Repeat
steps 1 and 2 to view additional files. You can also double-
click on the **filename** in the Open File window (browse
box) that appears.

• **SHORTCUT** Click on the file in an open Drive Window, and
drag it to the **Viewer** desktop icon.

• **OPTIONS–FILE MENU**

Open Opens a Browse window from which you can select a
file to view.

Close Closes the file in the active window.

Exit Closes the File Viewer window.

• **OPTIONS–VIEWER MENU**

Set Default Viewer Changes the translator for the next file
you select to view. If the file has an extension recognized as the
default by Norton Desktop, it will be opened in the recognized
format. If not, the program will attempt to open the file in the
translation specified here.

Set Current Viewer Changes the file translation for the active window. For example, if you have a text file in the active
window, select **Hex Dump** to see the file in a hexadecimal
translation.

• **OPTIONS–SEARCH MENU**

Find Searches for a text string or data that you specify. Key
in the characters you want searched for and click on **OK**. The
program will search the active window for that string and stop
when it is found.

Find Next Searches for the next occurrence of the string
specified.

Find Previous Searches backward in the active window for the previous occurrence of the specified string.

GoTo When you are viewing a spreadsheet or database, brings up the GoTo dialog box to let you input a specific row and column or field and record for the program to find.

• OPTIONS–WINDOW MENU

Cascade Arranges the open file windows in stair-steps with the title bars showing and the active file on top.

Tile Arranges the open windows so that all are visible. The amount of space allotted to each window diminishes as the number of open files increases.

Arrange Icons Adjusts the positions of the icons in mini-mized file windows.

Close All Closes all the open file windows but leaves the Viewer window open.

• **NOTE** At the bottom of this menu there is a list of all the open files with a check mark designating the active window. If you have more than nine files open, click on **More Windows** to see a complete list. When you click on More Windows, the Select Window appears, with a drop-down list inside. You can double-click on the **filename** to make it active, or highlight the filename and select **OK**. To make another file the active window, use the mouse to select the filename.

Part Three

Running Quick Access

By default, Quick Access runs under Norton Desktop. You can, however, configure it to run as a stand-alone program as well. If you installed Norton Desktop to run as your Windows shell, you must return to Program Manager in order to run Quick Access as a stand-alone program.

To Run Quick Access as a Stand-Alone Program

1. Using a text editor, open the Windows system.ini file.

2. Check to make sure that the shell= line reads

    shell=drive:\windows\progman.exe

    Key in this path, if necessary.

3. Save the file. After you do this you can run Quick Access from the DOS prompt by keying in

    win qaccess.exe

● **NOTE**   Quick Access can also be started from inside Windows by selecting Run… from the Program Manager's File menu and keying in **qaccess.EXE**. Be sure to include the path.

To Run Quick Access as Your Windows Shell

To run Quick Access as your Windows shell, replacing Program Manager, follow these steps:

1. Using a text editor, open the Windows system.ini file.

2. On the line shell=, enter

    shell=drive:\ndw\qaccess.exe

3. Save the changed system.ini file and restart Windows.

ARRANGING THE DESKTOP

The appearance of your Group windows can be defined in several ways. Group windows can display their icons in two styles as shown in Figure III.1. In the list style, items are arranged in a list down the window. Next to each item is the title and any additional description. In the icon style, the icons are arranged in rows with the title below each icon. The icon style is the display pattern used in Windows' Program Manager.

To Choose the Group Window Display Style

1. Select **View As**... from the Window menu.

2. In the View As dialog box, the name of the active group is shown next to Group. You can select either the **Icon** or the **List radio button** in the View Group As box. This choice will affect only the active group unless you also click on the **check box** for Change All Groups.

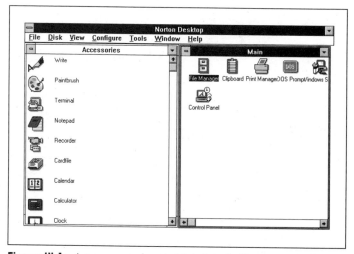

Figure III.1: A group window in List style (left): group window in Icon style (right)

3.   When you have made your choices, click on **OK**.

To Cascade or Tile Windows

1.   From the Window menu, select **Cascade (Shift-F5)** *or* **Tile (Shift-F4)**.

2.   Tiled windows will appear as shown in Figure III.2. An example of cascaded windows is shown in Figure III.3.

To Arrange Icons

Icons can be arranged manually or automatically. You can click on an icon and drag it to its new location, or you can rearrange icons by one of the following methods:

- Select **Arrange Icons** from the Window menu. Norton Desktop for Windows will automatically arrange the icons in the active window into neat rows. To save the new arrangement, see *Saving Changes* at the end of this section.

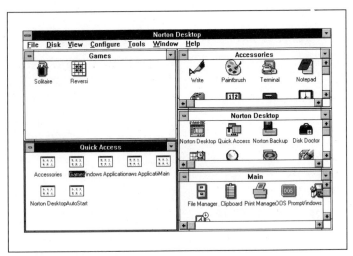

Figure III.2: Tiled windows

- Select **Quick Access**... from the Configure menu of Norton Desktop. Check the Auto Arrange Icons check box. Quick Access will arrange the icons whenever you resize the window or add an icon to the window.

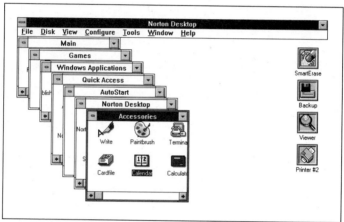

Figure III.3: Cascaded windows

AUTOSTART

If you want one or more group items to be launched when you start Quick Access, you can add them to the AutoStart group. For example, you can have your desktop organizer and spreadsheet program automatically started when you begin a work session.

To Add an Item to AutoStart

1. Select **AutoStart** from the Window menu or from the Quick Access group.

2. Open the **window** that contains the object you want to add.

3.   Click and drag the **object** to AutoStart. When you open
Quick Access, each item in the AutoStart window will
launch in its own application window.

● **NOTE**   To copy an item to AutoStart you must hold down the
Ctrl **button** while clicking and dragging.

CONFIGURE QUICK ACCESS

Settings for the Quick Access windows can be established through
the Configure menu of Norton Desktop.

To Configure Quick Access Windows

1.   Select **Quick Access**... from the Configure menu. The
dialog box Configure Quick Access will open as shown in
Figure III.4.

2.   The top box is called Default Group View. Select either
Icon View or **List View**. This will establish the display for
new windows you create. It will not affect current windows. To change existing windows, open **View As**... from
the Window menu.

3.   In the Settings box there are two check boxes and one text
box as follows:

● **Auto Arrange Icons**   This is a toggle to turn on
Quick Access' automatic rearrangement of icons when
a window is resized or has objects added to it.

● **Minimize on Use**   When checked, this causes the active window to be iconized on the desktop whenever
you launch an application.

- **Name of Main Group**   In this text box you will see
  the default name for the Quick Access main group
  which is Quick Access. To change the name, key in a re-
  placement name of up to 26 characters.

4. When you have made your choices, select the **OK** button.

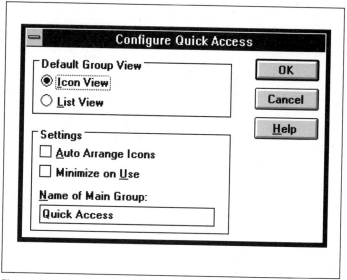

Figure III.4: Configure Quick Access dialog box

OBJECTS

Quick Access uses the term *object* to encompass both groups and
group items. If you open a group, its group window opens. If you
open a group item, that program will launch and open any file that
is included in that group item's definition.

CREATING NEW OBJECTS

When you make a new group, it is added to the collection of groups in Quick Access. When you make a subgroup, it is added to the active group. A new group item is added to whatever group is active when the group item is created.

To Create a New Group

1. To create a subgroup in an existing group, open the **existing group** and click on it to make it active. To make a top level group, make the Quick Access main group active.

2. Select **New** from the File menu.

3. Select the **Group radio button** in the Type box.

4. In the Title text box, key in the **name** you want to appear on the title bar of the new group. This name will also appear under its icon in the Quick Access window.

5. Key in a **Group File Name** if desired. Click on the **Browse button** to search through the drives and files for existing group filenames.

6. Include a description and a shortcut key if you want them.

7. The current icon for the group is shown at the top of the dialog box. To select a different icon, click on the **Icon button**. (See *To Change an Object's Icon* later in this section.)

8. Click on the **Password button** to assign a password and to restrict access to the group. (See *To Maintain a Password* later in this section.)

9. Click on **OK** when finished.

To Create a New Group Item Using the Mouse

1. Open a Drive Window for the drive with the program or file you want. Use the directory tree and File Panes to locate the file. (The drive icons are not available if you are running Quick Access as a stand-alone program.)

2.   Open the group window that is to be the new object's
      destination.

3.   Click on the **program** or **filename** and drag it to its des-
      tination window. The icon for that program or document
      will now appear in the group window.

• **NOTE**   To make a launchable icon, you can use a program file
with the extension .EXE, .COM, .BAT, or .PIF, or a document with a
file extension that is associated with an application. See *Associate a
File Extension with a Program* in "Managing Files," Part I.

To Create a New Group Item

1.   Select the **group** to which you want the item assigned.

2.   Select New… from the File menu. This will open the New
      dialog box as shown in Figure III.5.

3.   In the Type box, select **Item**. The object will become a
      group item icon in the active window.

4.   In the Title text box, key in the object's title. The title will ap-
      pear under the object's icon in the window (if you are using
      the icon display style) or next to the icon (if you are using the
      list display style).

      You can also leave this blank and Quick Access will assign
      a title using either the application name or the document
      name (for a document associated with an application).

5.   In the Program/Document/Script text box, key in the
      name of the **file** you want executed when this group item
      is opened. If you also want to open a particular document
      with the program, press the **space bar** once and then key
      in the document **filename**.

6.   In the Startup Directory, key in the path for the directory
      that Quick Access is to switch to when this object is open.
      If you do not include this information, your program may
      not be able to find all the files it needs in order to run.

7.   Key in a description and specify shortcut keys if you
      want them.

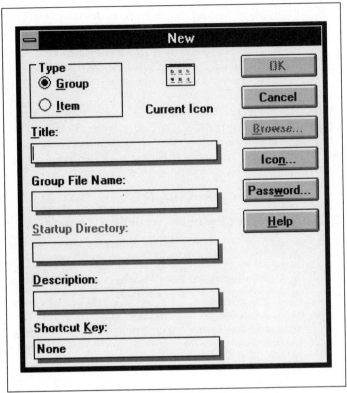

Figure III.5: The New dialog box for adding a new object

8. To change the default icon, click on the **Icon button**. (See *To Change an Object's Icon* below). Select the **Password button** to set a Password. (See *To Maintain a Password* later in this section).

9. Click on **OK** when finished.

● **NOTE** In the Program/Document/Script text box you do not need to include the full directory path for the application if the path is part of your AUTOEXEC.BAT file or the application is in one of the following directories:

- the Windows directory
- the Windows System directory
- the current directory

CHANGING OBJECTS

All the properties of an object, its directory path, icon, title, shortcut keys, and so forth can be changed at any time after the object's creation.

To Change an Object's Icon

1. For an existing object, select the **object** by clicking on it once. Choose **Properties**... from the File menu. Click on the **Icon button**.

2. For a new object, select the **Icon button** in the New dialog box, as described in *To Create a New Group* or *To Create a New Group Item* earlier in this section.

3. The Choose Icon dialog box opens as shown in Figure III.6.

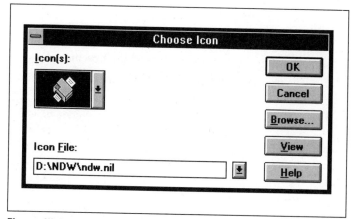

Figure III.6: The Choose Icon dialog box

4.   Click on the **prompt button** for the Icon(s) drop down box to see the icons available in the current file, which is shown in the Icon File text box. If you want to use one of the icons shown, click on it.

5.   If you want to see the icons in a different file, key in the name of library file and click on the **View button**.

or

Click on the **Browse button** to open the Select an Icon source file dialog box. Highlight a file and double-click on it to return the file and its path to the Icon File text box. Click on the **View button**.

6.   Highlight the icon you want in the Icon(s) box and click on **OK**. Click on **OK** again in the Properties box to confirm your choices.

To create your own icon, or to edit an existing one, choose **Icon Editor**... from the Configure menu. (See *Icon Editor* in "Tools and Utilities," Part IV.)

● **SHORTCUT**   A more direct route to the Choose Icon dialog box is to drag an icon from its group window to the desktop and, by clicking once, open the icon's control menu. Select **Icon**... from the Control menu. (See *To Turn on the Drive/Tool Icon* in "Configuring the Desktop," Part VI.)

To Maintain a Password

1.   For a new item, select **Password** in the New dialog box.

2.   For an existing item, select **Password** from the Properties dialog box.

3.   In the Password text box, key in any combination of letters and numbers up to 20 characters long. The password appears as a series of asterisks to keep anyone from seeing it as you key it in. Click on **OK**.

4.   You will be asked to confirm the password by keying it in again. After you key in the password a second time, press

Enter or select **OK**. Note that if the second password entry does not match the first, no password will be set.

• **NOTE**   Be sure to save your password using Save Configuration in the Configure menu or by turning on the Save Configuration on Exit check box in Preferences in the Configure menu. If you do not save your password, it will be in effect only for the current session of Quick Access.

To Disable a Password

1. If an object is password-protected, you will need to provide the password in order to open the Properties dialog box.
2. In the Properties dialog box, select **Password**.
3. Key in the current password and press **Enter** or click on OK.
4. When prompted for the new password, select **OK** or press **Enter**. Repeat this procedure in the Confirm Disable Current Password dialog box. Select **OK** in the Properties box to confirm the change.

To Change an Object's Properties

1. Select the object.
2. Select **Properties**... from the File menu.
3. The Properties dialog box will open. Except for its title, this box is identical to the New dialog box described in *To Create a New Group* and *To Create a New Group Item* earlier in this section.
4. Change existing properties or add new ones. Select **OK** when finished.

• **NOTE**   Properties that cannot be changed will appear dimmed in the Properties box. You cannot change any properties of the Quick Access main group except its title. (See "Configure Quick Access," Part III.)

To Delete an Object

1. Select the object to be deleted.

2. Select **Delete**... from the File menu.

3. A warning box appears asking you to confirm the deletion. If you are deleting a group, the warning box advises you that the group and all its items and subgroups will also be deleted.

4. Verify your selection and click on **Yes** to carry out the deletion.

● **SHORTCUT**   You can also delete an object by highlighting it and pressing the **Delete** key.

● **NOTE**   Deleting a program or document from the desktop or from a group does not delete the files from your disk. The icon will be removed, but the underlying files will remain.

To Move or Copy an Object Using the Mouse

1. Open both the object's current window and the window to receive it.

2. To move the object, click and drag it from its current window to the new window. To copy the object, hold down the **Ctrl** key while dragging the object.

To Move or Copy an Object using the Keyboard

1. Select **Move**... (**F7**) or **Copy**... (**F8**) from the File menu.

2. In the From box, highlight the item you want to move or copy.

3. In the To box, highlight the destination group.

4. Click on **OK** when finished, or **Cancel** to abandon the operation.

OPENING OBJECTS

There are four ways to open a group window and three ways to open a group item.

To Open a Group Window

Do *one* of the following procedures:

- Select the **group icon** and press **Enter**.
- Double-click on the **group icon**.
- Select the **icon**, then choose **Open** from the File menu.
- Select the **group** from the list in the Window menu. If more than seven windows are available, click on **More**... to see the entire listing in a scroll box window. Choose the group from the list and open it either by double-clicking on its **name**, or highlighting its name and selecting **OK**.

To Open a Group Item

Do *one* of the following procedures:

- Select the **group item icon** and press **Enter**.
- Double-click on the **group item icon**.
- Select the **icon** and choose **Open** from the File menu.

SAVING CHANGES

Two methods of saving changes are available. If you use Save Configuration from the Configure menu, your desktop will consistently reopen arranged as it is when you choose Save Configuration (until you save another configuration). This reopening arrangement will not change, no matter how the desktop looks when you exit.

If you choose the Save Configuration on Exit option, your desktop
will reopen looking the same as it did when you last exited.

To Save a Configuration for Future Sessions

1. Arrange your desktop exactly as you want.

2. Select **Save Configuration** from the Configure menu. If
   you are running Quick Access as a stand-alone, choose
   Save Configuration from the Options menu.

To Save the Configuration Just Before Exiting

1. To save the configuration that exists when you exit, select
   Preferences... from the Configure menu.

2. In the Preferences dialog box, toggle on the Save Configuration on Exit check box. Click on the **OK** button. If
   you are running Quick Access as a stand-alone, open the
   Options menu and toggle on Save on Exit.

Part Four

Tools and Utilities

BATCH BUILDER

Norton Desktop For Windows Batch Builder program is a text editor much like the Windows Notepad; however, it is designed to edit Windows Batch files that have the extension .WBT. These files are used by Norton's Batch Runner in much the same way that .BAT files are used by DOS. The Batch Builder includes a reference (*i.e*, an on-line help system) to the Windows Batch Language (WBL) which allows you to highlight a WBL command, see its syntax and an example, and import it directly into the batch file you are editing or building.

To Create a Batch File

1. Open the Batch Builder either by selecting **Batch Builder** from the Tools menu or double-clicking on the **Batch Builder icon** in the Norton Desktop group window.

2. Select **New** from the File menu, and key in the commands for the batch file.

3. Select **Save** or **Save As** from the File menu. The Save File dialog box will open. Key in a name for the file, including a .WBT extension. Click on the **OK** button, or press **Enter** to save the file.

● EXAMPLE

To create a batch file to open WordPerfect 5.1, and load the file "DAILY.LOG" in which you keep your work notes, open the Batch Builder, and key in the following line:

Run("WP.PIF","DAILY.LOG")

Then select **Save** or **Save As** from the File menu, and key in a name for the batch file, for example, "DAILYLOG.WBT". Select **OK** to save the file. Now, you can open a Drive Window and drag the file "DAILYLOG.WBT" onto the desktop. Whenever you want to open your log, just double-click on the **icon**.

To Edit an Existing Batch File

1. Open the Batch Builder either by selecting **Batch Builder** from the Tools menu or double-clicking on the **Batch Builder icon** in the Norton Desktop group window.

2. Select **Open** from the File menu, and then select the file to edit by highlighting the filename and selecting **OK** or double-clicking on the **filename**.

3. Edit the batch file.

4. Select **Save** from the File menu.

• EXAMPLE

To make the batch file that opens our daily log file a bit more intelligent, let's edit it. Open the Batch Builder, and then open the file "DAILYLOG.WBT". Edit it so that it reads like the following:

```
If WinExist("WordPerfect") == @TRUE Then Goto ACTIVATE
Run("WP.PIF","DAILY.LOG")
Goto END
:ACTIVATE
WinActivate("WordPerfect")
:END
```

Then select **Save** from the File menu. Now, when you double-click on the "DAILYLOG.WBT" icon that you put on the desktop, the batch file is smart enough to check to see whether you are already running a copy of WordPerfect, and if you are, to simply switch to it, instead of trying to open it again, which would result in an error message.

• OPTIONS

Undo   Recovers from the last Editor command.

Cut   Moves the currently selected text into the clipboard, deleting it from the current document.

Copy   Copies the currently selected text into the clipboard, without affecting the document.

Paste   Places the contents of the clipboard into the current document at the cursor.

Delete   Deletes the currently selected text. (Note that an immediate Undo will recover text that has been deleted, but it will not be copied to the clipboard.)

Select All   Highlights the entire document to make cut and paste operations easier.

To Search for Text

The Batch Builder has a basic search utility, although it does not support search and replace operations.

1.   Select **Find** from the Search menu. The Find dialog box opens as shown in Figure IV.1.

2.   Key in the text that you want to find into the Find text box. The previous selection will be highlighted automatically.

3.   Select **OK** to begin the search, or **Cancel** to abandon it.

● OPTIONS

Match Upper/Lowercase   When checked, limits the search to an exact case match.

Forward   Searches in the forward direction from the cursor.

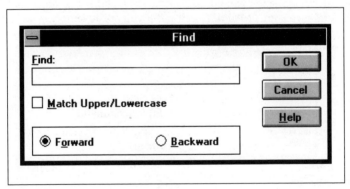

Figure IV.1: The Find dialog box

Backward   Searches in the backward direction from the cursor.

Find Next   Searches for the next occurrence of the current text to be found in the forward direction from the cursor.

Find Previous   Searches for the next occurrence of the current text to be found in the backward direction from the cursor.

To Insert a Batch Command into the Current Batch File

The Batch Builder has a built-in Reference manual that allows you to point to a command and insert it directly into your batch file.

1.   Select the **Reference!** menu.

2.   The Reference window shown in Figure IV.2 opens.

3.   Scroll through the alphabetical list of WBL commands in the Command scroll box.

4.   Highlight the command that you want to insert into the batch file. A description of the command, including its syntax and an example, will appear in the Description box.

5.   Double-click on the command, or select **Add** to add the command at the current cursor position, and return to the current batch file.

6.   Select **Close** to close the Reference window, or click on the main editor window.

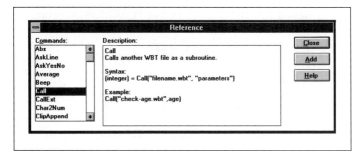

Figure IV.2: The Reference window provides an on-line Reference manual

CALCULATORS

Two calculators are included with Norton Desktop for Windows. The ten-key calculator is useful for financial calculations and to keep running totals. It also includes a tape function. The scientific calculator can do simple arithmetic calculations as well as more advanced functions such as logarithms, factorials, and exponents.

USING THE TEN-KEY CALCULATOR

After opening the ten-key calculator, you can click on the **minimize button** to iconize it. The calculator will be immediately available on your desktop.

To Open the Ten-Key Calculator

1. Choose **Calculator** from the Tools menu or double-click on the **Tape Calculator icon** in the Norton Desktop window.

2. The last calculator you used will open. To toggle between the ten-key and the scientific calculator, click on the Calculator menu. If the scientific calculator is open, select **Tape.**

3. The ten-key calculator, as shown in Figure IV.3, can be operated from the keyboard or by using mouse clicks. Table IV.1 lists each calculator key, the keyboard strokes necessary to access the key, and the function of the key.

To Change the Default Settings

1. Select **Setup** from the calculator's File menu. The Setup dialog box opens as shown in Figure IV.4.

2. Make your selections.

3. Click on **OK** when finished.

● SETUP OPTIONS

Notation is the setting for decimal places. The default setting is two decimal places.

Tax Rate is the sales tax percentage added to your total when you select the TAX key. Key in the **tax rate** you want to use.

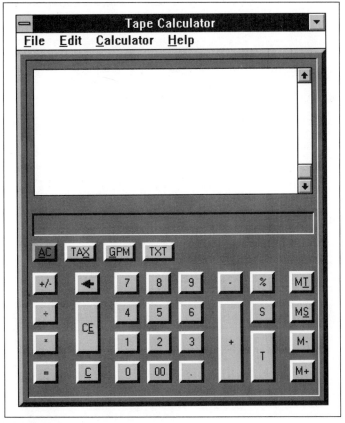

Figure IV.3: The tape calculator

Table IV.1: Keyboard Functions on the Ten-Key Calculator

Key	Keyboard	Function
AC	Ctrl+A	Clears all memory and keyboard registers
TAX	Ctrl+X	Calculates tax
GPM	Ctrl+G	Calculates gross profit margin
TXT	Shift+"	Turns text entry on and off
+/–	\	Changes sign
÷	/	Divides by the next entry
×	*	Multiplies by next entry
=	=	Equals
CE	Ctrl+E	Clears entry in the single-line display
C	Ctrl+C	Clear
–	–	Subtract
+	+	Add
%	%	Calculates percent
S	Shift+Enter	Subtotal
T	↵	Totals
MT	Ctrl+T	Totals and clears memory register
MS	Ctrl+S	Subtotals memory register
M–	Ctrl–	Subtracts current entry from memory. From the keyboard M– is Ctrl+–.
M+	Ctrl+	Adds current entry to memory. From the keyboard M+ is Ctrl++.

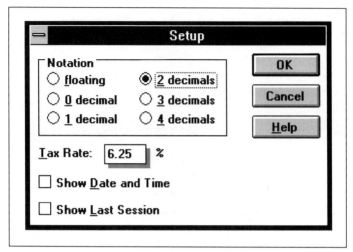

Figure IV.4: The Setup dialog box for the ten-key calculator

Show Date and Time if toggled on, puts the current date and time on each calculation.

Show Last Session if toggled on, displays the contents of your last work session when you start the calculator.

To Clear Your Data

- To clear a single display line, use the **Backspace** key or click on **CE**.

- To clear the memory register only, click on the **MT** key.

- To clear all transactions since your last total, click on **C**.

- To clear all registers and the tape, click on **AC**.

To Copy to Another Windows Document

1. From the calculator's display, highlight the total to be copied. The total must be in the calculator's display line.

2. Choose **Copy** from the calculator's Edit menu.

3. Select your Windows document. Position the cursor where you want the answer placed.

4. Choose **Paste** from the Edit menu of the document's application.

To Copy from Another Windows Document

1. In the Windows document, select the numbers you want and choose the **Copy** command.

2. Select the calculator you need.

3. Choose **Paste** from the Edit menu. It is not necessary to clear the display first. The number will not appear on the display line until you enter an operator (+, −, * and so forth.)

To Edit Your Entries

The tape display makes it possible to edit entries long after they have been made, even after they have scrolled off the screen.

1. Use the scroll bar to move to the entry that you want to change.

2. Double-click on that entry.

3. Enter the new number and click on the **operator** for the new number.

If the entry is in the Memo field, make sure the TXT function is toggled on. If the entry is on the active line, simply backspace to remove the number(s) or text, if the TXT function is on.

To Open a Tape File

1. Select **Open Tape**... from the calculator's File menu.

2. Key in the **filename** to the File text box or use the drive, tree, and file lists to locate the file that you want.

3. Select **OK** when finished.

To Print a Tape

1. If you want to print a different tape than the tape being displayed, choose **Open Tape**... from the calculator's File menu and follow the steps in *To Open a Tape File*.

2. Select **Print Tape** from the calculator's File menu.

To Save a Tape File

1. Select **Save Tape As**... from the calculator's File menu.

2. Key in the tape **filename** in the File text box.

3. Click on **OK** when finished.

To save changes to a tape file, choose **Save Tape** from the calculator's File menu.

USING THE SCIENTIFIC CALCULATOR

The Norton Desktop for Windows Scientific Calculator is a sophisticated calculator with 100 registers of storage, a full set of trigonometric and scientific functions, and the ability to work with hex and octal numbers. It uses the Reverse Polish Notation method and stacks to handle more complicated calculations easily.

Reverse Polish Notation and Stacks

Conventional arithmetic places the operators between the operands, which works fine for simple calculations, but breaks down with more complex ones. The Norton Desktop for Windows Scientific Calculator uses a four-element stack to handle "parentheses" formulas. A stack is a "Last In First Out" memory function. Reverse Polish Notation (RPN) when used with a stack provides a simple but elegant solution. With RPN, you enter the operands, and then the operator.

● EXAMPLES

$17 + 25 - 4 = 38$

Keystroke	Display
17	17
ENTER	17
25	25
+	42
4	4
−	38

$35 \div (3 + 2) = 7$

Keystroke	Display
35	35
ENTER	35
3	3
ENTER	3
2	2
+	5
/	7

The Mechanics of the Scientific Calculator

You can use the mouse to select all the keys and functions on the calculator, or you can use the keyboard or a combination of the two. To use the mouse, simply click on the **button**. To access the functions above each button, first click on the **ALT** button. At the top of the calculator the ALT legend will be visible, as shown in Figure IV.5. Press the **button** below the function you want. To use the keyboard, use the numbers and functions on the numeric keypad for number entry. For other functions, the key to use is capitalized and underlined in the display. For example, the cosine function is the C key. To access the functions above each button, tap the **Alt** key first, then press the **letter** that is capitalized.

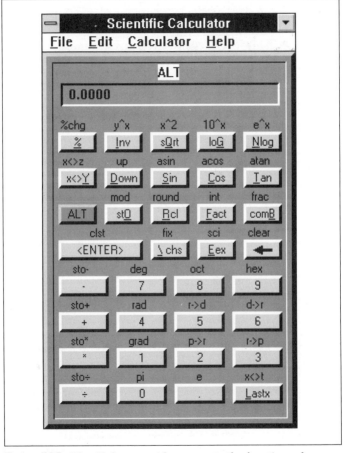

Figure IV.5: The Alt key provides access to the functions above the buttons

To Display a Fixed Number of Decimal Places

The display can be set to a fixed number of decimal places. To set to three decimal places follow these steps:

1. Click on the **ALT** button first; then click on the \ **chs** button, which is underneath *fix*.

2. Click on the **3** button.

To Display in Scientific Notation

The display can also be set to scientific notation, with a fixed number of decimal places. To set to scientific notation with two decimal places:

1. Click on the **ALT** button, then click on the button below *sci*, the **Eex** button.

2. Click on the **2** button.

To Display the Hex or Octal Equivalent

The hexidecimal or octal equivalent of the current integer value can be displayed. Note, however, that only the integer portion is displayed. The decimal fraction is truncated.

1. Click on the **ALT** button, then click on the button below *hex*, the **9** button. The hex equivalent of the integer portion is displayed. For octal, click on the button below *oct*, the **8** button.

2. To return to the previous display, click on the **ALT** button again, then click on the Backspace key.

• EXAMPLE

Key in the number **16**, and press the **Enter** key, or click on the **ENTER** button. The display shows

16.0000

Tap the **Alt** key, or click on the **ALT** button, then press the **9** key or click on the **button** below *hex*. The display shows

10

which is 16 in hexadecimal notation. Then tap the **Alt** key again, and press the **8** key, or click on the **button** below *oct*. The display changes to

20

which is the octal equivalent of 10 hex or 16 decimal.

Functions

The scientific calculator has approximately 50 different mathematical and trigonometric functions, depending on how you count them. Each can be accessed with the keyboard, the mouse, or both. A complete listing of the functions and keystrokes is given in Table IV.2.

Table IV.2: The Functions of the Scientific Calculator

Button	Keyboard	Function
	Ctrl+Ins	Copies display (x register) to clipboard
	Shift+Ins	Pastes clipboard to display (x register)
ALT	Alt	Enables Alt-mode functions
	F1	Help
%	%	Calculates x percentage of y register
%chg	Alt,%	Calculates percent difference between x and y registers
+	+	Adds y register to x register
−	−	Subtracts x register from y register

Table IV.2: The Functions of the Scientific Calculator (cont.)

Button	Keyboard	Function
×	*	Multiplies y register by x register
÷	/	Divides y register by x register
←	Backspace	Deletes last digit in display
Enter	↵	Pushes value in display into y register, y register into z register, z register into t register, t register is deleted
\ chs	\	Changes sign of display (x register)
10^x	Alt,G	Calculates 10 to the xth power
acos	Alt,C	Calculates arc cosine of x register
asin	Alt,S	Calculates the arc cosine of x register
atan	Alt,T	Calculates the arc tangent of x register
clear	Alt,Backspace	Clears x register, or clears hex/octal display
clst	Alt,↵	Clears stack (x, y, z, and t registers)
comB	B	Calculates the combinations of y register, x register at a time
Cos	C	Calculates the cosine of x register
d–>r	Alt,6	Converts x register from degrees to radians
deg	Alt,7	Displays angles as degrees
Down	D	Scrolls stack downward

Table IV.2: The Functions of the Scientific Calculator (cont.)

Button	Keyboard	Function
e	Alt,.	x = Euler's constant(2.718…)
Eex	E	Inputs exponent of 10 (scientific notation)
e^x	Alt,N	Computes the natural exponent of x register
Fact	F	Calculates the factorial of the x register (x!)
fix	Alt,\	Displays in fixed decimal notation
frac	Alt,B	Fractional portion of x register
grad	Alt,1	Uses gradients
hex	Alt,9	Displays integer portion of x register in hexadecimal (base 16)
int	Alt,F	Integer portion of x register (truncates x)
Inv	I	Calculates the inverse of x register (1/x)
Lastx	L	Replaces x register with previous value of x register
loG	G	Calculates the logarithm of x register
mod	Alt,O	Returns the modulus of x/y (the remainder)
Nlog	N	Calculates the natural logarithm of x register
oct	Alt,8	Displays integer portion of x register in octal (base 8)

Table IV.2: The Functions of the Scientific Calculator (cont.)

Button	Keyboard	Function
p–>r	Alt,2	Converts x register, y register from polar to rectangular coordinates
pi	Alt,0	x = pi (3.14159…)
r–>d	Alt,5	Converts x register from radians to degrees
r–>p	Alt,3	Converts x register, y register from rectangular coordinates to polar coordinates
rad	Alt,4	Changes display from degrees to radians
Rcl	R	Recalls contents of register 00-99 to register x
round	Alt,R	Rounds the x register to nearest whole number
sci	Alt,E	Selects display in scientific notation
Sin	S	Computes sine of x register
sQrt	Q	Calculates square root of x register
stO	O	Stores contents of x register in register 00-99
sto+	Alt,+	Adds contents of x register to contents of register *nn* and stores in register *nn*
sto–	Alt,–	Subtracts contents of x register from contents of register *nn* and stores in register *nn*
sto×	Alt,*	Multiplies contents of x register by contents of register *nn* and stores in register *nn*

Table IV.2: The Functions of the Scientific Calculator (cont.)

Button	Keyboard	Function
sto÷	Alt,/	Divides contents of register *nn* by contents of x register and stores in register *nn*
Tan	T	Calculates the tangent of x register
up	Alt,D	Scrolls stack upwards
x<>t	Alt,L	Swaps contents of x register and t register
x<>Y	Y	Swaps contents of x register and y register
x<>z	Alt,Y	Swaps contents of x register and z register
x^2	Alt,Q	Squares value of x register
y^x	Alt,I	Raises y register to power of x register

DISK DOCTOR

The Disk Doctor program runs numerous tests on your disk drives to monitor problems in the Partition Table, DOS Boot Record, File Allocation Table (FAT), and the directory and file structures. It also checks your drives for lost clusters and cross-linked files.

Disk Doctor should be used in the following situations:

- when you have trouble accessing a disk or when a disk behaves erratically;

- when files or directories seem to be missing but were not deleted;

- when you want to practice preventive maintenance to look for budding problems.

To Use the Disk Doctor

1. Select **Disk Doctor** from the Tools menu or double-click on the **Disk Doctor icon** in the Norton Desktop group window.

2. Click on one or more **drives** in the Select Drives box. The program starts running as soon as you click on the **OK** button. The name of the drive being diagnosed will appear in the Title bar. As the Disk Doctor moves through the tests, the Fill bar tracks the progress being made for each test. If you selected a floppy disk drive, a window appears with the message:

Insert the Diskette to diagnose into Drive A: or B:

3. To halt the program, click on the **Pause** button which will then change to a Continue button. Click on the **Continue** button to start up the program again. To stop the program, first select **Cancel** and then select the **Exit** button.

When the tests have been completed, a list of those tests will be displayed. Select **Info...** for a detailed report that can then be saved and/or printed.

If an error is found, the Disk Doctor will display a message reporting the nature of the problem and describing the reason it should be repaired. Problems found by the Disk Doctor can be corrected by exiting Windows and using the Norton Disk Doctor (NDD) program included on the Emergency Diskette. See Appendix C, "Using the Emergency Diskette," for instructions on using the Emergency Diskette.

What the Disk Doctor Tests

Partition Table   Shows DOS how to find the partition(s) on your hard disk. If the Partition Table is damaged, DOS will not be able to access the hard disk.

Boot Record   Contains information about the disk's characteristics (size, layout, and so forth). If the record is corrupted, DOS cannot read the disk.

File Allocation Table (FAT)   Tells DOS how to find all the
sectors belonging to a file. If the FAT is damaged, DOS will not
be able to locate one or more files.

Directory Structure   Shows DOS how to find files on the
disk. If the directory structure is corrupted, entire directories
may be lost.

File Structure   Tests each file's directory entry against its
FAT mapping and ensures that they agree.

Lost Clusters   Checks for clusters that contain valid data but
cannot be linked to a known file.

DISK LABEL

Labeling a hard disk is a security measure designed to prevent accidental formatting. The format program in Norton Desktop for
Windows and the regular DOS format will not format a labeled
hard disk unless the label name is provided.

To Add or Change a Disk Label

1. Select **Label Disk** from the Disk menu.

2. In the dialog box, click on the **prompt button** to see a list of
the drives on your system and their assigned labels, if any.

3. Select the drive and key in the **label name** in the New
Label text box. Select **OK** when finished.

To Delete a Disk Label

1. Select **Label Disk** from the Disk menu.

2. Click on the **prompt button** and select the drive.

3. Use the mouse to highlight the name in the New Label text box. Press **Delete**. Select **OK** when finished.

DISKETTE FUNCTIONS

Norton Desktop for Windows allows you to format and copy diskettes inside the Windows environment. All the diskette functions that are new in DOS 5.0 are available here in a graphical, easy-to-use form.

To Format a Diskette

1. Select **Format Diskette** from the Disk menu.

2. Click on the prompt buttons at the side of the drop down boxes to select one option from each of the following windows:

   Diskette   Select the A: drive or B: drive.

   Size   Select the size of the diskette being formatted.

   Format Type   The *Safe* format uses its own formatting algorithm which allows the recovery of data (using Un-Erase) in the event of accidental formatting. The *Quick* format is very fast because it only rewrites the FAT table on the diskette and thus cannot be used on a previously unformatted diskette. A *Destructive* format is the same as a DOS format and erases the data completely and irrevocably. If you are formatting new unformatted diskettes, you must use the Destructive format.

3. Select any options that you want. Click on **OK** when you have made your choices. Select **OK** or **Cancel**.

● OPTIONS

Make Disk Bootable   Transfers DOS system files to the diskette so your computer can boot from them.

Volume Label   If desired on the diskette, may be keyed in here.

● **NOTE**   Save Unformat Info saves information necessary to reverse the format in case of accidental formatting. You must use the Save Unformat Info option for the Quick Format Type if you want to be able to UnErase the diskette.

To Copy a Diskette

1.   Select **Copy Diskette** from the Disk menu.

2.   Click on the **prompt buttons** to select the source and destination drives. Click on **OK**.

3.   You will be prompted to insert the source diskette. Click on **OK**.

4.   You will then be prompted to insert the target diskette. If the target diskette is already formatted or contains files, a window opens with a warning message. Select **OK** if you want to go ahead. Select **Swap** if you want to change target diskettes, or **Cancel** to abandon the operation.

5.   When you are finished copying, you will be asked if you want to make another copy of the source diskette. Select **Yes** if you do, **No** if you want to exit.

● **NOTE**   A diskette can be copied only to a diskette of identical configuration. If you attempt to copy a diskette of one capacity to a diskette of a different capacity, you will get an error message.

ICON EDITOR

The Norton Icon Editor is a complete icon management tool. It lets you work with individual icon files, the icons inside executable files, and libraries of icons. With the Icon Editor, you can perform the following tasks:

● Create or change existing individual icons.

- Create, change, or replace program icons.
- Create, delete, or change individual icons in icon libraries.
- Create or change entire icon libraries.

ABOUT ICONS

Both Windows and Norton Desktop For Windows use icons to provide a visual way to identify programs. Icons can be stored as individual .ICO files, within the application program file itself, or in icon libraries. By default, Norton Desktop For Windows uses icon libraries with the .NIL extension. The Norton Icon Editor lets you edit and work with icons in all three places.

Icons can be associated with an application program, or with any object in the desktop.

THE ICON EDITOR

To start the Icon Editor, select **Icon Editor** from the Tools menu or double-click on its icon in the Norton Desktop for Windows group. The Icon Editor will look like the one shown in Figure IV.6.

Parts of the Icon Editor

The parts of the Icon Editor are as follows:

PART	FUNCTION
Workspace	The Workspace is the main area of the Icon Editor. It consists of a 32 by 32 grid, each square of which represents a pixel in the icon.
Icon display	The Icon display shows the current icon in the Workspace, including all edits.

PART	FUNCTION
Tools palette	The Tools palette contains eight tool buttons with the drawing tools that are used to edit the icon in the Workspace. Click on one of the **tool buttons** to select its tool.
Brush Size palette	The Brush Size palette has four buttons for selecting different brush sizes. The four available sizes are these: 1 pixel by 1 pixel; 2 pixels by 2 pixels; 3 pixels by 3 pixels; 4 pixels by 4 pixels.

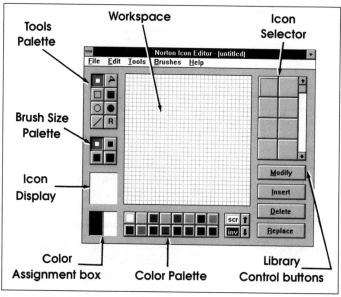

Figure IV.6: The Icon Editor

PART	FUNCTION
Color Assignment box	The current color assignments for the right and left mouse buttons are shown in the Color Assignment box. An *s* or an *i* in the box indicates that it is a screen color or its inverse. If neither an *s* nor an *i* appears, that indicates that it is a "fast" color. (See *How To Select Colors* later in this entry.)
Color palette	The Color palette shows the available colors. At the right of the palette there are the Screen Color box and the Inverse Color box, and two Spin buttons which cycle through the colors. The Screen Color box shows the current screen color while the Inverse Color box shows a pre-assigned contrasting color.
Library Control buttons	The four Library Control buttons are Modify, Insert, Delete, and Replace. They are used to move icons to and from the Workspace and to insert or delete icons from a library. When editing individual icons or executable files, only the Modify and Replace buttons are available.
Icon Selector	The Icon Selector is a scrollable box with eight buttons displaying the icons in the library or executable file.

THE DRAWING TOOLS

The drawing tools are used to edit the icon in the Workspace. The eight tools are shown in Figure IV.7. They are as follows:

TOOL	FUNCTION
Brush	The Brush tool allows you to change the color of the pixels in the Workspace either by clicking on the pixel, or by dragging the pointer over an area. The size of the brush is controlled by the Brush palette, and the color of the brush is controlled by the Color palette.
Filler	The Filler tool fills a region with the color assigned to the left or right mouse button. It will fill a contiguous area which includes the pixel on which you click.
Rectangle	The Rectangle tool draws an outline of a rectangle in the Workspace. Click on one corner of the rectangle and then drag the pointer to the opposite corner.
Filled Rectangle	The Filled Rectangle tool works the same as the Rectangle tool, except that the inside region of the rectangle is filled with the assigned mouse button color.
Circle	The Circle tool draws an approximation of an ellipse inside an imaginary rectangle. Click on one corner of the imaginary rectangle and then drag the pointer to the opposite corner.
Filled Circle	The Filled Circle tool works the same as the Circle tool, except that the inside region of the ellipse is filled with the assigned mouse button color.

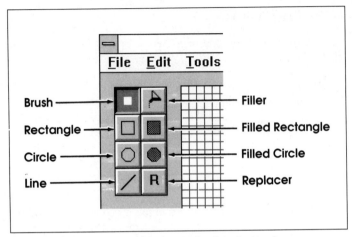

Figure IV.7: The Tool Palette has eight drawing tools

TOOL	FUNCTION
Line	The Line tool draws a line in the Workspace. Click on one end of the line and then drag the pointer to the end of the line.
Replacer	The Replacer tool works like the Brush tool, except that it replaces all the pixels of one color with another color. The replacement color is the color assigned to the button used, and the color replaced is the color assigned to the other button. This tool is very handy for changing one color without affecting any of the different colored pixels around it.

HOW TO SELECT COLORS

There are two kinds of colors in the Icon Editor: Screen and Inverse colors and Fast colors. Screen and Inverse colors can be changed by using the two Spin buttons to cycle through the palette. Fast colors do not change once they have been painted.

- To set the left mouse button to a Fast color, move the cursor to the color on the Color palette and click on the **left mouse button**.

- To set the right mouse button, repeat the procedure.

- To set a mouse button to a Screen color, move the cursor to the scr button and press the **mouse button**.

- To set a mouse button to the Inverse color, position the cursor on the inv button and click on the **mouse button**.

- To change the Screen and Inverse colors, click the **left mouse button** on one of the **spin buttons** to the right of the scr and inv buttons. These cycle through the color pairs in opposite directions.

WORKING WITH INDIVIDUAL ICONS

Norton Icon Editor allows you to work with individual icons. You can create new icons either by modifying an existing icon and saving it to a new filename, or by creating the new icon from scratch. This new icon can then be saved as an individual icon, or as part of a library of icons.

To Create an Icon

1. Start Norton's Icon Editor by double-clicking on its **icon**, or by selecting **Icon Editor** from the Tools menu. If you are already in the Editor, select **New** from the File menu.

2. If you selected New from the File menu, a dialog box will open. Select **Icon** to work on an individual icon.

3. The Workspace will clear, and the Brush tool will be selected.

4. Draw the icon.

5. Click on the **Replace button** to move the icon in the Workspace to the Icon Selector.

6. Select **Save** or **Save As** from the File menu to save the icon in an .ICO file, or a .NIL file if you are creating a new library (and if you chose Icon Library in step 2 above).

• **NOTE**   To undo any changes made to the icon in the Work-space since the last time you changed tools, select **Undo** from the Edit menu.

To Edit an Existing Icon

1. Start Norton's Icon Editor by clicking on its **icon**, or selecting the **Icon Editor** from the Tools menu. Select **Open** from the File menu.

2. Select the **icon** to be edited.

3. Click on the **Modify button** to move the icon into the Workspace and then select the drawing tools and colors desired.

4. When you have finished editing the icon in the Workspace, click on the **Replace button** to overwrite the original.

5. To save the modified icon in an individual .ICO file, select **Export Icon**, **Save**, or **Save As** from the File menu. Selecting Export Icon or Save will cause a dialog box to appear. Key in the **filename** for the modified icon and then select **OK**.

    Warning: Selecting Save will result in overwriting the original icon with the one now in the Workspace.

WORKING WITH ICON LIBRARIES

Norton Desktop For Windows allows you to create and work with libraries of icons. Working with icons in these libraries is similar to working with individual icons, except that you can add or delete icons from the libraries, and import or export icons to individual .ICO files.

To Import an Icon

1. Open the library that you want to modify by selecting **Open** from the File menu. The Open dialog box will be displayed.

2. Select from the File Type box whether to import an icon from an existing library file, an executable file, or an individual icon file.

3. Select the **file** from which to import.

4. Select the **icon** to import from the Icon Selector button bar near the bottom of the dialog box.

5. Select **OK** to import the icon to the Icon Editor's Workspace, or **Cancel** to cancel the operation.

To Export an Icon

1. Move the **icon** to be exported to the Icon Editor Workspace.

2. Select **Export Icon** from the File menu.

3. The Export Icon dialog box will open. Key in the **filename** for the icon.

4. Select **OK** to save the icon to an .ICO file, or **Cancel** to cancel the operation.

To Delete an Icon from an Icon Library

1. Click on the **icon** to be deleted in the Icon Selector.

2. Click on the **Delete button**. The icon will be delete immediately from the Icon Selector.

3. Select **Save** from the File menu to make the change permanent.

To Insert an Icon in an Icon Library

1. Open the Icon Library to insert an icon into the library, or select **New** from the File menu to start a new library.

2. Draw the icon to be inserted in the Workspace, or import it from another file, using the **Import Icon** from the File menu.

3. Click on the **Insert button**. The icon in the Workspace will be inserted into the library in front of the current icon.

4. Select **Save** from the File menu to make the change permanent.

WORKING WITH ICONS IN EXECUTABLE FILES

An icon or icons can be embedded in executable files. Norton's Icon Editor allows you to change these icons, or to replace them with icons of your own. You cannot, however, change the number of icons in the executable file.

To Edit an Icon in an Executable File

1. Select **Open** from the File menu.

2. Select the **Executable** radio button.

3. Select the **file** to edit.

4. Select **OK** to bring the file into the Icon Editor, or **Cancel** to cancel the operation.

5. Select the **icon** to change in the Icon Selector.

6. Click on the **Modify button** to move the icon to the Workspace.

7. Edit the icon.

8. Click on the **Replace button** to replace the icon with the edited icon in the Workspace.

9. Select **Save** from the File menu to make the changes permanent.

To Replace an Icon in an Executable File

To replace an icon in an executable file with one from another source, such as an icon library, follow the first five steps from *To Edit an Icon in an Executable File,* above. Then follow these steps:

1. Select **Import** from the File menu.

2. Select the **file** and **icon** to import to the Workspace. (See *To Import an Icon* above).

3. Click on the **Replace button** to replace the icon with the icon you imported to the Workspace.

4. Select **Save** from the File menu to make the changes permanent.

KEYFINDER

The KeyFinder is a handy utility that allows you to find the keystrokes to insert special characters into your current Windows application quickly and easily. You can use either the keyboard or a mouse, or a combination of both. To start KeyFinder, either select **KeyFinder** from the Tools menu, or double-click on its **icon** in the Norton Desktop for Windows group window. You will see the default KeyFinder window, as shown in Figure IV.8.

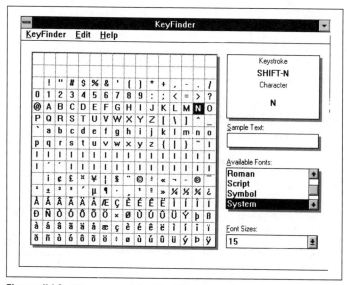

Figure IV.8: The parts of the KeyFinder window

The KeyFinder window is composed of the Character Table, arranged in either rows or columns, the Keystroke Information box, the Sample Text box, the Available Fonts box, and the Font Size box.

To Find a Character Code

1. Choose the font. (See *To Change Font* below.)

2. Click on the **character** or **symbol** desired.

3. The character will be displayed in the Keystroke Information box, along with the keystroke(s) used to create it.

● EXAMPLE

To find the keystrokes for the copyright symbol, in the System font, select the **System font** in the Available Fonts box, then click on the © symbol. The copyright symbol is displayed in the Keystroke Information box, along with the keystrokes to create it in the System font, which is Alt 0169.

● **NOTE** To key in extended ASCII characters (those greater than the ASCII code of 127) into most Windows applications, first make sure that the NumLock is on. Then hold down the **Alt** key while entering the number shown in the Keystroke Information box. Release the **Alt** key.

To Insert Multiple Characters into the Current Windows Application

1. Select the **font** being used by the application in the Available Fonts box. (See *To Change Font* below.)

2. Select the **characters** to insert into the application by double-clicking on them. They will appear in the Sample Text box.

3. Highlight the characters in the Sample Text box by dragging across them with the mouse.

4. Copy the characters to the clipboard. Select **Copy** or **Cut** from the Edit menu. Alternately, press **Ctrl-Insert** to copy the characters or **Shift-Delete** to cut them to the clipboard.

5. Change to the application.

6. Paste them into the application. This is usually **Shift-Insert**.

● **NOTE**   The actual keystrokes are pasted into the application, not the formatted characters. Make sure to select the font and size being used before performing the paste operation.

● **OPTIONS–EDIT MENU**

Lower Case   Changes all the characters in the Sample Text box to lower case.

Upper Case   Changes all the characters in the Sample Text box to upper case.

Copy Cell   Copies the current cell in the Character Table into the Sample Text box. This has the same effect as double-clicking on the cell.

To Change Font

1. Click on the scroll bar arrows until the desired font becomes visible.

2. Click on the font name. The Character Table will change to show the new font.

To Change Font Size

1. First select the font in the Available Fonts box.

2. Click on the **prompt button** of the Font Size box to show the available font sizes.

3. Scroll through the font sizes and select the one desired. This will be the size shown in the Keystroke Information box, if Real Font Size is toggled on.

• OPTIONS–KEYFINDER MENU

Swap Orientation   Changes the Character Table from a row orientation to a column orientation.

Real Font Size   Shows the actual size of characters in the Keystroke Information box.

Show ASCII   Shows ASCII code for nonprinting characters.

Sample Text   Toggles the Sample Text box display.

Programmer Mode   Changes the Keystroke Information box to show additional information about the character selected, including the following details:

- the keystroke
- the character
- the decimal equivalent for the character
- the hex equivalent for the character
- the octal equivalent for the character
- the type of font selected
- the font style selected

Programmer Mode also changes the Character Table to show a hex number grid on the outside, and eliminates the Font Size box. See Figure IV.9.

SCHEDULER

The Scheduler allows you to run programs and display messages at preset times and organizes these tasks on an events list. For example, when you first install Norton Desktop for Windows you are asked if you want to run an automatic backup of files at 4:00 pm every day. If you answer Yes, the Scheduler starts up with a Daily Backup ready to run.

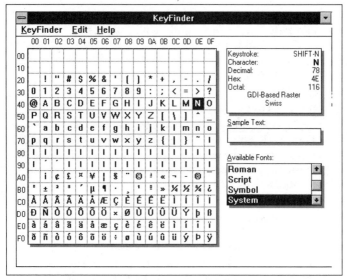

Figure IV.9: The Programmer Mode shows additional useful information for programmers

To Add an Event to Scheduler

1. Select **Scheduler** from the Tools menu or double-click on the **Scheduler icon** in the Norton Desktop group window.

2. Click on the **Add button** to see the Add Event window as shown in Figure IV.10.

3. Key in a description of the event in the Description box. This is the text that will appear on the events list.

4. Select **Run Program** or **Display Message**. Key in the command line to execute or the message to display.

5. Set the time and date for the event to take place. When finished, click on **OK**.

• OPTIONS–ADD EVENT AND SCHEDULER

Run Program Select this **radio button** and the Scheduler will launch any Windows program, non-Windows program, DOS command, or batch file.

Command Line to Run   Enter a command line of up to 128 characters, or select your program by using the Browse button. The Scheduler will launch any file that has an extension-application association. (See "Associate a File Extension With a Program" in Part Two.)

Run Minimized   Causes the scheduled program to run minimized rather than full screen.

Display Message   Select this **radio button** to display a message at a scheduled time. Enter the message in the Message to Display box. At the prescribed date and time, the message will appear on your screen and a beep will sound. The message remains on the screen until you click on **OK**.

Schedule Frequency   Events and messages can be scheduled in the following categories: one time, hourly, weekdays, weekly, or monthly. The various scheduling boxes activate or dim-out depending on the category chosen.

Hide When Iconized   When the Scheduler is minimized, this causes the icon to be hidden, though still active. To reopen the Scheduler, select from the **Tools** menu or double-click on the **Scheduler** icon in the Norton Desktop window.

Load With Windows   Modifies the Windows WIN.INI file to automatically load Scheduler when Windows starts. Check this box if you have any events scheduled for daily, weekly, or monthly intervals.

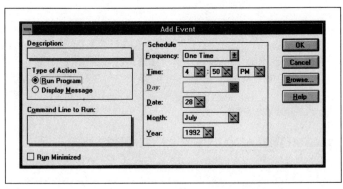

Figure IV.10: The Add Event window in Scheduler

To Edit, Copy, or Remove Events

1. Open the Scheduler and use the mouse to highlight an event.

2. Click on **Edit** to modify the details of an event. Click on **Copy** to place a copy of the event on the main list. Click on **Delete** to delete the event from the list.

● **NOTES** The Scheduler must be active for messages to appear or for programs to be launched. Turn on the **Load With Windows** box in the **Scheduler** for the program to be loaded automatically when Windows starts.

Events will not be launched while you have the Add Event or Edit Event window open in Scheduler. Until you finish and minimize the window, Scheduler will be disabled.

You can change the display of dates and times by altering the International settings in the Windows Control Panel.

SHREDDER

Shredded files are deleted permanently from your system. Unlike files removed with the Delete command, they cannot be retrieved using UnErase. By default, the Shredder overwrites the selected file with zeroes.

To Shred a File or Subdirectory

1. To bring up the Shredder dialog box, do one of the following:

 • Double-click on the **Shredder icon** on the desktop.

 or

 • Double-click on the **Shredder icon** in the Norton Desktop group window.

 • Select **Shredder** from the Tools menu.

2. Key in the name of the file or directory to be shredded. If you are not sure of the location of the file you want to shred, click on the **Browse button** to scan drives and directories for file-names. Click on **Include Subdirectories** to shred files in subdirectories and the subdirectories themselves.

3. Click on **OK**. A warning box will pop up twice for each file and subdirectory with the reminder that shredding a file is permanent. If you want to proceed, click on **Yes** in each warning box.

● **SHORTCUT** Click on a **filename** in a Drive Window and drag the file's icon to the Shredder icon on the desktop.

● **WARNING** Be careful not to shred more files than you intend. Shredded files are destroyed permanently and cannot be recovered by any normal means.

● **NOTES** To designate a shredding pattern other than the default, select **Shredder** from the Configure menu and pick a pattern from the following:

US Government Shredding Overwrites the file using a government standard shred using decimal character 246 as the last character. This method causes the file to overwrite repeatedly and is significantly slower than the normal default method which overwrites using zeroes.

Use Special Over-Write Pattern Allows you to specify a decimal value from 0 to 255 to use as a file overwrite pattern. The use of a special pattern does not slow the shredding process.

Repeat Count Specifies the number of times the file will be overwritten.

Sophisticated data recovery devices *may* be able to recover data unless you have used the US Government Shredding method. Normal means, such as using UnErase or other data recovery utilities, will not be able to recover shredded files regardless of the shredding method chosen.

SLEEPER

The Sleeper is a screen-saver package that protects your monitor screen by displaying a constantly moving image when you are not actively using your computer. Sleeper also includes password protection to prevent anyone from clearing the screen saver and accessing the screen on which you were working.

Choosing a Screen-Saver Graphic

1. Select **Sleeper** from the Tools menu or double-click on the **Sleeper icon** in the Norton Desktop group window.

2. Click on the **Enable check box** in the bottom right corner of the Sleeper dialog box to activate the program. The default for Enable is "on."

3. Select a **graphic** from the scrolling box on the left side of the screen. When you click on a choice, configuration options, if any, will appear in the center box.

4. Click on the **Sample button** to see a display of the image you chose. Use the scroll bars and check boxes in the sample window to adjust the image.

5. Select the **Restore button** to return to the main Sleeper dialog box.

• OPTIONS–CHECK BOXES

Hide When Iconized When selected, will cause the Sleeper icon to disappear. The program will remain active but to review or change Sleeper options you must select **Sleeper** from the Tools menu or double-click on the **Sleeper icon** in the Norton Desktop group window.

Load With Windows Changes the Windows WIN.INI file to load the Sleeper program whenever Windows is started.

Enable Turns the Sleeper program on and off.

• OPTIONS–PREFERENCES

Time Trigger Boxes   Causes the screen-saver graphic to appear after a set period of time without input from the keyboard or mouse. The default setting is five minutes, but you can set it to appear at any interval, from ten seconds to 999 minutes and 59 seconds.

Sleep Now Corner   Selects a corner that will immediately activate the Sleeper function when the mouse pointer is moved there.

Sleep Never Corner   Overrides the time set in the Time Trigger boxes when you move the cursor to the selected corner and prevents the screen-saver graphic from appearing.

Use Sleep Corners   Turns the Sleep Corners on and off.

Use Sleep Hot Keys   Enables the use of keyboard hot keys to turn the screen-saver graphic on.

Select Hot Keys   Place the cursor in the text box and select a single key or two keys in combination to act as an immediate activator of the screen-saver graphic. Your choice of Hot Key(s) will appear on the main Sleeper dialog box in the lower-left corner. If the Use Sleep Hot Keys check box is not selected, the entry in the Select Hot Keys text box will be dimmed-out and the Hot Key on the main Sleeper dialog box will show as undefined.

• **NOTE**   Choose hot keys carefully. If you pick a combination that duplicates a key combination in Norton Desktop for Windows or Windows, you may cause a conflict in your system.

• OPTIONS–PASSWORD

No Password   No password required. This is the default setting.

Use Network Password   Requires the network password, if you have one, to wake up the screen.

Custom Password   Allows you to choose a password that will be required to wake up the screen. Key in the password and click on **OK**. Asterisks will appear in the box to prevent anyone from looking over your shoulder and seeing your password, so a second box asks you to enter the password again.

● **NOTE**   The password protects only the screen that you were looking at before the screen saver activated. It does not protect your system files which can be accessed simply by rebooting.

● OPTIONS–WAKE UP

Wake On Key Strokes   Screen wakes up when any key is pressed.

Wake On Mouse Clicks   Screen reappears when a mouse button is clicked.

Wake On Mouse Movement   Causes the screen-saver graphic to disappear when the mouse is moved.

● **NOTE**   Sleeper must be active in order to run. You can load it by selecting it from the **Tools** menu and then clicking on the **Mini-mize** box. A more convenient way is to click on the **Load With Windows** option described above. If you close the Sleeper, it becomes inactive.

SMARTERASE AND UNERASE

Using the SmartErase and UnErase combination you can provide many levels of protection for your files. With SmartErase enabled you can be sure of being able to recover all deleted files within the limits of parameters you set. Files that have been marked for protection are saved by SmartErase in a hidden directory called *Trashcan*. Recovery of files from the Trashcan directory is both swift and certain.

In order for SmartErase to be enabled, you must have the line

ep /on

in your AUTOEXEC.BAT file. This line should be immediately after your PATH statement. Norton Desktop for Windows will add the line to your AUTOEXEC.BAT at the time of installation if you choose. Even without SmartErase, you can usually recover deleted files using UnErase alone, provided you act promptly. UnErase is always enabled but file recovery is not guaranteed.

To Recover a File Using SmartErase

1. Select **UnErase** from the Tools menu or double-click on the **SmartErase icon** on the desktop. The SmartErase dialog box opens as shown in Figure IV.11.

2. Click on the **directory** or **subdirectory** in the left pane for the file you want to recover. Deleted files will be listed in the right pane. Files with the first character changed to a question mark are unprotected files deleted by DOS. These files may be recoverable if unerased promptly.

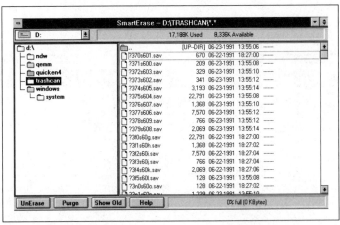

Figure IV.11: The SmartErase/UnErase dialog box

3. Select the file you want to recover and click on the **Un-Erase button**. The file will be recovered, removed from the Unerase window and restored to its original position.

4. If the file is one that was deleted while unprotected, you will see a new dialog box with the message

> **DOS has overwritten the first letter of the filename. Please provide a new first letter.**

Enter a new first letter for the filename and select **OK**. The file has now been recovered. If the file is not recoverable, you will see an error message.

● OPTIONS–SMARTERASE/UNERASE

Purge   Removes designated files from the SmartErase window and from the Trashcan directory. Files that are purged are no longer protected by SmartErase.

Hide Old/Show Old   Toggles display to show or hide old files, including duplicate entries and entries that were deleted long ago.

● SHORTCUT   Use the **Tab key** to highlight the directory or file window and begin keying in the name of the directory or file you want. The highlight cursor will move to the first entry that matches your keystrokes.

To Configure SmartErase

To conserve disk space, you may not want to have SmartErase preserve every file that has been deleted, or you may want to limit the time that SmartErase protects deleted files.

1. Select **SmartErase** from the Configure menu.

2. Select the drives you wish to protect. From the options offered, enter the parameters for the files you wish protected and choose the storage limits you want.

3. Click on **OK** to accept your choices or **Cancel** to abandon the operation.

• OPTIONS–SMARTERASE

Enable SmartErase Protection   If this line is dimmed-out, it means that the erase protection program (ep /on) is not installed in your AUTOEXEC.BAT. If the box is checked, it can be selected and cleared to disable SmartErase.

Drives and Files to Protect

Click on the drives you want to protect. SmartErase will create a Trashcan directory on each protected drive. The default is all hard drives on your system.

All files   Protects all files on the drives selected.

Only the files listed   Select this **radio button** to protect only certain types of files, then list up to nine file extensions in the File Extensions text box. These extensions must be separated from each other by a space or comma.

All files except those listed   Protects all files except those whose extensions are listed in the File Extensions text box.

Protect archived (backed up) files   Protects files that have not been changed since their last backup. The default is off because it is presumed that these files, if accidentally deleted, could be recovered from backup disks.

• OPTIONS–SMARTERASE STORAGE LIMITS

You can select either a storage time limit or a size limit or both.

Time   Select the **Purge Files Held Over X Days** check box. Enter the number of days that you want the files protected. The possible range is from one day to 99. If this box is selected without also selecting the Size box, the Trashcan directory may become very large, taking up too much space on your hard disk.

Size   Fill in the amount of disk space that you want allotted to protected files in the line Hold at Most X Kbytes of Erased Files. If you choose this check box, the minimum size you can set for the Trashcan directory is 16 Kb and the maximum size is 9,999 Kb. When the size limit is reached, SmartErase will purge the oldest files from the Trashcan.

SUPERFIND

SuperFind can search for a specific file or for files that match a specific pattern, such as all files with the letters MEMO in their filenames, or all files with a .TXT extension. SuperFind can also perform a text search for files that contain the text for which you are looking.

Using the combination boxes and the More button, your search can be defined in a number of ways: according to the filename, extension, location on the drive, and even the time of day the file was created.

To Start SuperFind

Use one of the following procedures:

- From Norton Desktop, select **SuperFind** from the Tools menu.

- From the Norton Desktop group window, double-click on the **SuperFind icon**.

To Search for a File

1. Key in the name of the file, including any extension, in Find Files or click on the **arrow** next to the Find Files combination box to see default choices.

2. In the Where box, key in the path to be searched or select an option from the combination box.

3. Click on **Find**. The Directory line at the bottom of the dialog box shows the progress of the search. Files matching the criteria in the Find Files box will appear in a SuperFind Drive Window below the dialog box. Each subsequent search will produce a new Drive Window unless you toggle on Reuse Drive Window in the Options menu.

To Search for Text in a File

1. Key in the range of files and areas to be searched in the Find Files and Where boxes. If you want to search all files, click the **prompt button** on the Find Files combination box and select **All Files**.

2. In the With Text box, key in the text string that you want to find. The total amount of text, including spaces, must be no more than 30 characters. For an exact match, including upper and lower case letters, select **Match Upper/Lower-case** in the Options menu. Your four most recent text searches can be seen by clicking on the With Text **prompt button**.

3. When you have filled in all the search parameters, click the **Find button**.

● OPTIONS–SUPERFIND–THE FIND FILES BOX

All files   Same as the *.* file specification.

All files except programs   Searches for all files except those with .EXE, .COM, and .BAT extensions.

Documents   Finds all .DOC, .TXT and .WRI files.

Database files   Searches for all dBase compatible files (.DB?) and all Q&A data files (.DTF)

Programs   Finds files with program extensions: .EXE, .COM, and .BAT.

Spreadsheet Files   Finds all Lotus (.WK?) and Excel (.XLS) worksheets.

● **NOTES**   You can use the standard DOS wildcards of * and ? to specify files in the Find Files box, plus the pipe (|) which represents one or zero characters.

You can search for several types of files at once by separating each file specification with a delimiter character: comma(,), semicolon(;), plus sign (+), or a space.

To exclude a file type from your search, precede it with a minus sign (–).

● EXAMPLES

! ! !.*   Searches for all filenames with three or fewer characters.

LET*.*   Searches for all filenames beginning with the characters LET.

.TXT,.BMP   Searches for all .TXT and all .BMP files.

. –.INI   Searches for all files except those with the .INI
extension.

● OPTIONS–THE WHERE BOX

Current drive only

All drives

All drives except floppies

Current directory and subdirectories

Current directory only

Floppy drives only

Local hard drives only

Network drives only

Path

● OPTIONS–THE MORE BUTTON

This button opens up the SuperFind window, as shown in Figure IV.12, so you can define your choices even further. With these
options you can set the following:

Attributes   These are tri-state boxes, three-way toggles. A blank
check box means the program will search only for files with attribute bit turned off. An X in the box means files must have this
bit on. A grayed box means the setting of the bit is ignored.

Date, Time, Size   By default, these boxes are set to Ignore.
Click on any of the **prompt buttons** to see the choices available.
When you select any one of these options, one or more text
boxes pop up for you to complete.

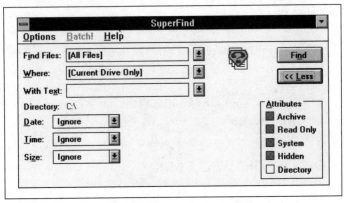

Figure IV.12: The expanded SuperFind window

To Set Up Search Sets

The default file and location search sets can be modified or deleted and new sets can be added up to a total of 16 file sets and 16 location sets.

1. Select **Search Sets** from the Options menu to see the Search Sets window shown in Figure IV.13.

2. Click on either the **File Sets** or **Location Sets button**.

3. To add a search set, click on **Add**. Key in the name of the set and the definition in the text boxes. Wild cards and delimiters, as defined above, can be used. Click on **OK** to confirm the addition. The new set will be added to the Search Sets list.

4. To edit or delete a set, highlight the set with the mouse and click on **Edit** or **Delete**. Click on **OK** to confirm the change.

● **WARNING** Use the Delete button with caution. The deletion will be made immediately without a warning notice. If you press delete in error, click on the **Cancel** button to save the deleted item.

To Create a Batch File from a File List

1. After SuperFind has found your file or files, select **Batch** from the Menu bar.

2. Key in a name for the batch file in the Save As box. Select the **Browse button** to browse for a directory in which to place the batch file.

3. Key in any batch instructions you want in the Insert Before Filename and Append After Filename text boxes. Select options that you want to include. Choose **Launch** to test the batch file in DOS. An error in the batch file will cause it to abort. To find the source of the error, toggle on PAUSE After Each Command to step through the batch.

4. Select **OK** to save the batch file.

• OPTIONS–BATCH FILES

Full Path   Select this option if files in the batch file are located in different directories. This will insert the full path name for each file in the batch file.

Spaces Around Filename   When this option is checked, blank spaces are entered automatically before and after the filename on each Command line of the batch file. The default is On.

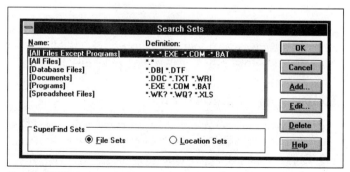

Figure IV.13: The Search Sets window

102   Tools and Utilities

CALL Each Command   When checked, this option will insert the batch language CALL command at the beginning of each line of the batch file.

PAUSE After Each Command   When toggled on, this command will insert a pause after each operation in the batch file. When launching a batch file you can then examine each command as it is executed.

See Also   Appendix B, "Batch Language"

• OPTIONS–MENU

Animation   Turns the animated search icon on and off. The search should be faster with Animation turned off.

Exclusive Search   Stops all other programs and prevents task-switching while the search is being performed. For faster searches, toggle this option on. To have searches performed in the background while you do other work, toggle this option off.

Minimized Search   Minimizes the window to an icon while conducting the search.

SYSTEM INFO

System Information displays and prints detailed reports of your computer's hardware and software characteristics, including benchmark comparisons of your system with other popular computers.

To Use System Information

1.   Select **System Info** from the Tools menu or double-click on its icon in the Norton Desktop group window.

2.   The System Summary window is displayed as shown in Figure IV.14. Click the **buttons** at the top of the window for the reports you want to see or select from the reports in the Summary menu.

3. To print one or more reports, choose **Report Options** from the File menu. Use the mouse to select the reports you want to print. Click on **OK**. Select **Print Report** from the File menu.

4. To save a report, choose **Save Report**... from the File menu. In the Save Report dialog box, you may select a directory by scrolling in the directory tree box. Double-click on your choice. Key in a **filename** in the File text box and click on **OK** to save the file.

● OPTIONS–SYSTEM REPORTS

System Summary   Provides detailed information about your systems's hardware and configuration, including network information, if appropriate.

Disk Summary   Initially displays a summary of all the hard drives. Click anywhere on a **summary line** to bring up a detailed Drive Window with information on the characteristics

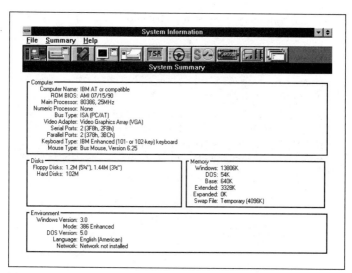

Figure IV.14: The System Summary window

of the drive such as the number of sectors, sectors per cluster, and so forth. When you select this report, a Window menu is added to the Menu bar so you can arrange and select the Drive Windows.

Windows Memory   Displays a graphical representation of the memory both used and unused in Windows.

Display Summary   Reports video type, technology, and capabilities. Use scroll bars to access the entire listing.

Printer Summary   Describes the characteristics and capabilities of your printer. If more than one printer is installed, the information is provided only for the one designated as active.

TSR Summary   Lists the terminate and stay resident (TSR) programs in memory. Includes information about size and addresses.

DOS Device Driver Summary   Shows the address, name, and description of the device drivers in memory.

Real Mode Software Interrupts   Addresses and owners of software interrupts. A complete understanding of interrupts is useful for diagnosing and correcting hardware and software conflicts.

CMOS Summary   Reports on the information contained in the battery-powered CMOS chip. This chip maintains data on the drives and memory that the computer needs when booting up.

Processor Benchmark   Tests the speed of your computer's central processor (CPU) and shows a bar chart comparing it to other popular computers.

Startup Files   Opens a pane for each of your startup files: the AUTOEXEC.BAT, CONFIG.SYS, WIN.INI, SYSTEM.INI, and NDW.INI files. A Window menu is added to the menu bar so you can switch between the panes and rearrange them.

Part Five

Norton Backup

Norton Desktop for Windows includes Norton Backup for Windows, a full-featured, flexible backup program that can be configured easily for novice or advanced users alike. Note that, unlike many backup programs, Norton Backup for Windows operates in the Windows environment, and can run in the background while you continue working on other tasks in the foreground.

● **WARNING!**   Do **NOT** attempt to run any other program that uses the floppy disk controller while using Norton Backup for Windows. Data loss and/or system crash are very likely to occur if another program tries to use one of the floppy drives while Norton Backup for Windows is running.

Before Norton Backup for Windows (NBW) can run on your computer, it needs to know what kind of floppy drives you have, and how your computer responds to certain commands. To get this information, the first time you start Norton Backup for Windows it will automatically run a series of tests to determine how your hardware operates, and it will check to make sure that its options are correctly set to ensure reliable backups. It is strongly recommended that you complete all of these tests before attempting to make backups, because there is no point in making undependable ones.

THE FIRST TIME

1. Click on the **Norton Backup for Windows icon,** or select **Backup** from the Tools menu.

2. Norton Backup for Windows will scan your initial hard drive (usually the C: drive) to obtain a list of directories and files.

3. An information box will pop up advising you that the compatibility tests have not been run yet. Select **OK** to proceed.

4. Another information box will open which will tell you that your floppy drives have not yet been configured. It will ask you if you want to configure the drives automatically. Select **Yes** to proceed.

5. Norton will try to determine automatically what kind of floppy drives you have on your computer. If it gets this

wrong (which it did with us), don't worry, just keep following the steps. You can fix the problem later. A message box will open which shows the configuration it found. Select OK to proceed.

6. Norton Backup for Windows will then display one message box that tells you it will perform two tests automatically, one test of the DMA (Direct Memory Access) and one of the Disk Change detection. It warns you that if the DMA test fails, your computer may crash and require a reboot. If that happens, don't worry, reboot your computer, and then restart Windows and Norton Backup for Windows. Norton Backup will recognize that your computer failed the DMA test and will set the DMA option to its slower and more compatible mode, and then continue the testing.

7. After the DMA test, Norton Backup then checks the Disk Change detection. An information box opens which instructs you to remove all disks from the floppy drives. Remove any disks, and click on **OK**.

8. A box opens telling you whether your computer has passed the test. Click on **OK** to continue.

9. Next, Norton Backup for Windows will run a small compatibility test. This test does a two-disk backup of files, and then compares the backed up files against the originals. Select **Start** to begin. A Warning box will pop up advising you not to allow any other programs to use the floppy drives during this test. Click on **OK** to proceed.

10. If Norton Backup for Windows incorrectly determined your floppy drive types earlier, this test will fail. Select **Cancel** to cancel the test, and then select the proper disk drive types.

11. Once the disk drives are correctly configured, select the **Compatibility Test button,** and run the compatibility test.

12. Follow the prompts to run the backup and compare. Note that if you change disks within 15 seconds of the initial prompt, Norton Backup for Windows will detect the change automatically.

ADJUSTING
CONFIGURATION

To open the Configure window click on the **Configure button** on the Button bar under the Menu bar. This will allow you to make changes to the program level, floppy drive type, disk logging method, catalog file path, and DMA speed. Note that changes made here apply to all operations within Norton Backup for Windows.

Also, if you change any of your hardware after the initial installation and running of Norton Backup, you should re-run the following configuration tests by clicking on the appropriate buttons.

● OPTIONS–CONFIDENCE TESTS

Auto Floppy Config   Reconfigures your floppy drives automatically.

Compatibility Test   Runs the two-disk backup and compare test to ensure dependable backups.

Configuration Tests   These tests the Fast DMA option and Disk Change detection.

● OPTIONS–PROGRAM LEVEL

Preset   All options within the Backup, Compare, and Restore windows are preset by the setup file, except the drive to back up to, or restore/compare from.

Basic   Allows limited access to changing options within the Backup, Compare, and Restore windows.

Advanced   Allows full access to all options within the Backup, Compare, and Restore windows.

• OPTIONS–FLOPPY DRIVES

- Not Installed
- 360 Kb 5¼
- 720 Kb 5¼
- 720 Kb 3½
- 1.2 Mb 5¼
- 1.44 Mb 3½

• OPTIONS–DISK LOG STRATEGY

Fastest   Works with most disk drives, but will not work with networked or substituted drives.

Most compatible   Works with all DOS devices and requires less memory than Fastest option.

• OPTIONS–OTHER

Catalog File Path   Key in the path to the location that you want Norton Backup for Windows to store its catalog files. By default, these are in the same directory as Norton Backup for Windows. They are also stored on the last disk in each set.

Slow DMA   This is a check box that will be set **on** if your computer fails the DMA test during initial startup.

THE BACKUP WINDOW

Norton Backup for Windows allows you a wide range of ways to handle backups. You can preconfigure your backups, and then run them automatically by adding parameters to the command line when you run Norton Backup, either by invoking it manually, or by starting it with the Scheduler automatically.

You can create a variety of predefined setup files that back up different groups of files, or you can interactively select the files to back up and then either store them in a new setup file, or not, as you wish.

In addition, you can control the number of possible options for each backup, from virtually none (except for choosing a predefined set of files with the program level set to Preset) to a full range of options for compression technique, format type, and so forth, with the program level set to Advanced. Or, finally, you can back up files by highlighting them in a Drive Window and dragging them to the Backup icon on the desktop.

TYPES OF BACKUPS

There are three basic types of backups. These are the following:

- Full
- Incremental
- Differential

In addition, there are copy versions of the Full and Incremental backup types which do not change the archive bit of the files that are backed up, nor do they affect the backup cycle settings. These two options are useful primarily as means of transferring files between computers, and will not be discussed again.

A Full backup is one made of all the files that you select. This can be all the files on the hard disk (a total backup), all the files in a particular drive or directory, or some other reasonable subset of the files on your hard disk. A Full backup turns off the archive bit on the files backed up, and it begins a backup cycle. You can save the set of files selected for backup for later re-use as a backup set.

An Incremental backup includes all the files in the set of files that have changed since the last Full or Incremental backup was done. An Incremental backup turns off the archive bit of each file that has been backed up. In the event of disaster, to restore all the files to your hard disk, you must restore the Full backup set, and *all* Incremental backup sets. Do not re-use incremental diskettes between Full backups, because a complete restore requires the full set plus *ll* the incrementals.

A Differential backup includes all the files in a set of files that have changed since the last Full backup was performed. A Differential backup does not turn off the archive bit. In order to restore files to your hard disk, you need only restore the last Full backup plus the most recent Differential backup. You can re-use all differential backup diskettes except the most recent, unless you want to maintain multiple versions of the changed files.

PROGRAM LEVEL

There are three program levels for Norton Backup for Windows: Preset, Basic, and Advanced. In the Backup window, these control the number and type of options that are available to the user. The program level is set in the Configure window.

• OPTIONS–PRESET

The only options available in the Backup window at the Preset level are the setup file to use, which is selected using the Preset Backups text box, and the drive to use, which is selected using the Backup To: drop down box.

• OPTIONS–BASIC

The Basic program level gives the user access to all the options at the Preset level, plus the ability to create or change setup files (see *Setup Files* below); create and run macros (see *Macros* in the *Automating Backup* section); change file selections (see *Selecting Files* below); change the Backup type (see *Types of Backups* above); and, additionally, the following toggles:

Verify Backup Data   When on, Norton Backup for Windows compares the source file and the backed up file. This slows the backup process, but greatly improves the confidence level.

Compress Backup Data   When on, Norton Backup for Windows compresses the files as they are backed up, saving disk space and reducing the time needed for the backup process.

Prompt Before Overwriting Used Diskettes   When on, if you insert a diskette that has been used before, Norton Backup for Windows will display an alert box. This allows you to replace the diskette with a new one, or to verify that it is alright to overwrite the current one.

Always Format Backup Disks   When on, Norton Backup for Windows will always format the backup disks, even if they are already formatted. This slows down the backups, but it also protects against disks that may have been formatted in drives whose heads were out of alignment.

Use Error Correction on Diskettes   When on, Norton Backup for Windows will write additional error correction information on the diskettes to provide an additional level of data integrity. Note, however, that this error correction information will use from 11–13 percent of the available disk space.

Keep Old Backup Catalogs On Hard Disk   When on, Norton Backup for Windows will keep old backup catalog files on the hard disk. This can be useful if you use backups to keep track of version information, and if you want to restore an older version of a file without having to rebuild the catalog from the disks.

Audible Prompts (Beep)   When on, Norton Backup will beep whenever an action is required on your part, or an error condition occurs. Note that this beep will not occur if you have "Beep=no" in your WIN.INI file.

Quit After Backup   When on, Norton Backup will automatically quit when the backup is completed.

• OPTIONS–ADVANCED

With the program level set to Advanced, all the options that are available at the Basic level remain available, with the following additions or changes:

Data Verification   There are three choices provided for data verification:

- **Read and Compare** which checks every byte;
- **Sample Only** which checks every eighth track;
- **Off** which does no checking.

Data Compression   There are four choices provided for the level of compression:

- **Off,** which does no compression,
- **Save Time** which does compression only while the Central Processing Unit (CPU) is idle, waiting for the floppy drive;
- **Save Disks (Low)** which tends to result in greater compression than Save Time, but runs slower on slow computers;
- **Save Disks (High)** which minimizes the amount of disk space used, but generally runs slower than the other options, except on the fastest computers.

Overwrite Warning   There are four levels of overwrite warning provided:

- **Off** which gives no warning before overwriting previously used diskettes;
- **DOS-Formatted Diskette** which warns you before overwriting any DOS diskette that contains data;
- **Backup Diskettes** which warns you before overwriting any diskette that contains Norton Backup data;
- **Any Used Diskette** which warns you before overwriting any diskette that contains any data at all.

Component Size   This option is available only when you are backing up to a DOS path. It allows you to choose the size of the backup file, which can make later transfers to diskette much easier. The options are the following:

- Best fit, which will use the maximum size available.
- 1.44 Mb
- 1.2 Mb
- 720 Kb
- 360 Kb

Proprietary Diskette Format   When on, Norton Backup for Windows uses a special diskette format that allows more data to fit on each diskette, but which may take longer and will make the diskettes uncopyable with DOS commands.

Full Backup Cycle   When on, Norton Backup will automatically switch from the regular Differential or Incremental backup
to a Full backup when it detects that the number of days
elapsed since the last Full backup is equal to the number in
this box.

SETUP FILES

Setup files are files that you create which define a group or set of files to
back up. For example, you could have a setup file that would be a total
backup of your hard disk. This set would include all drives and directories on your hard disk. Another set might hold all your word processing files, and would include all the files in your C:\WP51\FILES
subdirectory. Still another might be the files required for your monthly
newsletter, which could include some spreadsheet files, some word
processing files, some database files, and a Pagemaker file. Each of these
might have a different backup strategy associated with it. You might do
total backups only once a month, with weekly incrementals, for example, but do weekly Full backups of your word processing files, with
Differential backups on a daily basis. Your newsletter, on the other
hand, would get a Full backup once a month after you finish it, and
nothing in between.

To Open a Setup File

1. Click on the **Backup, Compare,** or **Restore button.**

2. Select **Open Setup** from the File menu. The Open Setup
    File dialog box will open.

3. Choose from the list of available setup files and select **OK**
    to open the file.

To Create a New Setup File

1. Click on the **Backup button.**

2. Click on the **Select Files... button.**

3. Select the files that you want to include in this backup set.
    For details on selecting files, see *Selecting Files* below.

4. When you have completed your file selection, select **OK** to return to the Backup window.

5. Select the type of backup you want this to be.

6. Select the destination for the backup (Backup To:).

7. Click on the **Options button.**

8. Select the options you want for this backup set.

9. Select **Save Setup As** from the Files menu.

10. Key in the new **filename** for this setup file. Be sure to include the .SET extension.

To Change an Existing Setup File

1. Click on the **Backup button.**

2. Open the setup file you want to modify, or select it using the **Setup Files drop down box.**

3. Make the changes you want to make to the file selection, backup type, backup device, and so forth.

4. Select **Save Setup** from the File menu to save the changes, or select **Save Setup As** to create a new setup file.

SELECTING FILES

There are many different ways to select files for backing up. The simplest way to select an individual file is to drag it from a Drive Window to the Backup icon on the desktop. For larger groups of files, though, it pays to create setup files that include all the options and files you want. See *To Create a New Setup File* above for instructions on how to create such a setup file.

To Select Backup Files

1. Click on the **Backup button** to open the Backup window.

2. Click on the **Select Files button** to open the Select Backup Files window. This window, which is shown in Figure V.1, has two panes, a Tree Pane and a File Pane, as well as a button bar at the bottom.

3. Select directories for backup by using one of the following methods:

- Double-click on the name of the directory in the Tree Pane to toggle the selection of its files on or off.

- Highlight the directory in the Tree Pane, and then press the **space bar** to toggle the selection of its files on or off.

- Highlight the directory in the Tree Pane, and then press the **Insert** key to select the files in that directory, or the **Delete** key to deselect the files in that directory.

4. You can select individual files in the File Pane using the same methods used in step 3 for directories.

5. If you are running at the Advanced program level, you can select groups of files meeting specific criteria using the Include, Exclude, and Special buttons in the button bar at the bottom of the window.

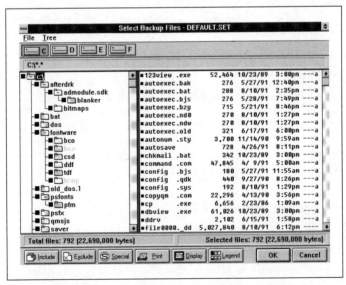

Figure V.1: The Advanced Select Backup Files window

6.   Save your selections by clicking on the **OK** button, or abandon them by clicking on the **Cancel** button.

• OPTIONS–BUTTON BAR

Include   The Include button, which is available only at the Advanced program level, opens up the Include/Exclude Files dialog box shown in Figure V.2. Fill in the path for files to include in the Path text box, and the file specification in the Files text box, and select the **Include radio button.** Check the *Include Subdirectories* box to include all subdirectories in the selection. Then click on **Add** to add this group of files to your selected files shown in the Include/Exclude List box. Highlight a description in the Include/Exclude List box and click on **Delete** to remove a group of files from the list. When you are done, choose **OK** to accept the selections, or **Cancel** to abandon them.

Exclude   The Exclude button, which is available only at the Advanced program level, also opens the Include/Exclude Files

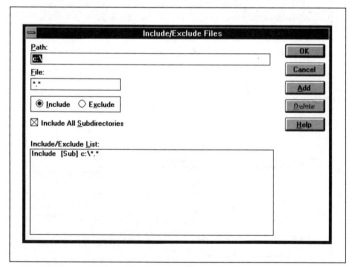

Figure V.2: The Include/Exclude File window

dialog box shown in Figure V.2. Everything works the same as with Include, except that the Exclude radio button is selected. Use this to exclude groups of files from being selected.

Special   The Special button, which is available only at the Advanced program level, opens the Special Selections dialog box shown in Figure V.3. This box allows you to select files to include by a range of dates, and to exclude special files such as copy protection files, hidden and system files, and read-only files.

Print   The Print button opens the Print File List box. This box allows you to print a list of files on the current drive or all files on your computer's drives. You cannot select individual files for inclusion on the list, and it ignores your current setup file. (*All* files are always printed.) You can choose to print using the graphics mode of your printer, or the straight text mode which is quicker. You can also choose to print to a file by checking the Print to File box, and entering the filename in the text box. Select **OK** to print the list, or **Cancel** to close the box without

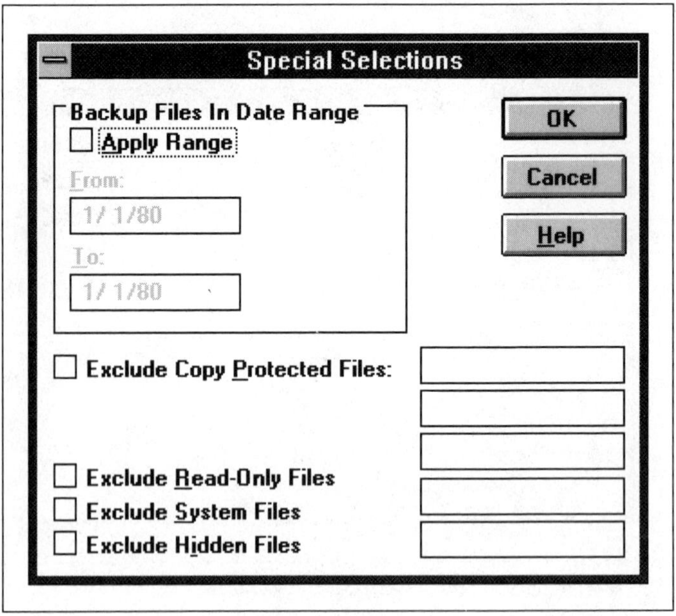

Figure V.3: The Special Selections window

printing. The Setup box may open either the Printer
Parameters dialog box for your printer, or an information box
telling you to use the Windows Control Panel, depending on
the type of printer selected.

Display   The Display button opens the Display Options dialog
box. With this box, you can choose the amount of information to
display about each file, the order in which files are displayed,
whether to group selected files together, whether the Tree and File
Panes are displayed side by side, or top and bottom, and whether
to show only certain files in the display (Filter).

Legend   The Legend button opens the Backup Selection
Legend box shown in Figure V.4. This box shows what the
selection icons in the Tree and File Panes mean.

• OPTIONS–MENU

File, View   Opens a View window to let you view the
contents of the highlighted file.

File, Delete   Allows you to delete the highlighted file.

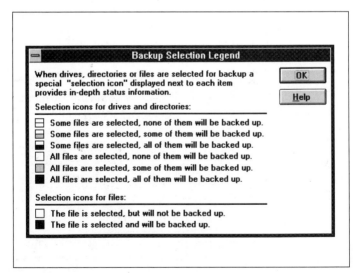

Figure V.4: The Selecting Files Legend window

File, Select All   Selects all the files on the current drive unless specifically excluded in the Special Selections dialog box.

File, Deselect All   Deselects all the files on the current drive.

Tree, Expand One Level   If there are subdirectories of the currently highlighted directory in the Tree Pane that are not visible, this shows them one level deeper for that branch.

Tree, Expand Branch   This expands the display in the Tree Pane to show all subdirectories of the currently highlighted directory.

Tree, Expand All   This expands the display in the Tree Pane to show all directories on the current drive.

Tree, Collapse Branch   This collapses the display in the Tree Pane to show no subdirectories below the currently highlighted directory for that branch.

● **NOTES**   Clicking on the icon in the Tree Pane will expand or contract the tree if there are subdirectories of that directory, but it will not select files for backup. You must double-click on the directory name to toggle file selection.

If there are *collapsed* branches of the tree *below* the currently highlighted directory (as shown by a plus sign (+) in the center of the directory icon), selecting or deselecting the current directory for backup will affect its hidden directories as well. If the tree is expanded, and the subdirectories are visible, then selecting or deselecting the current directory will not affect its subdirectories.

When creating a macro to automate file selection procedures, always use the Insert and Delete keys rather than the mouse or the space bar to select files.

Both the Tree Pane and the File Pane have a feature which, when you move the mouse pointer to the Legend box, causes an *i* to appear alongside the pointer. If you click once on the left mouse button, a message box appears:

Backup Directory Selection Information

This gives you information on the directory name, creation date, number of files in the directory, number of selected files, and the number of files to be backed up. If you are in the File Pane, it gives you information on the individual file.

THE COMPARE WINDOW

The Compare window allows you compare previously backed up files against the files currently on your hard disk. Use this to verify the integrity of a backup without actually restoring the files. To reduce the time it takes to do a comparison, you can select the files to compare so that you check only irreplaceable files.

To Compare Files

1. Click on the Configure button to open the Configure window.

2. Select the program level to use.

3. Click on the **Compare button** to switch to the Compare window.

4. Select the backup catalog to use.

5. Select the files to compare by clicking on the **Select Files button** and selecting the files in the Select Compare Files window.

6. Select the drive from which to compare.

7. If using the Basic or Advanced program level, select the location of the files with which you want to compare.

8. If using the Basic or Advanced program level, click on the **Options button** to set beeps on or off, and whether to quit after the comparison is completed.

9. If using the Basic or Advanced program level, and you want to use a catalog not on the default drive and directory, or you need to rebuild a catalog, click on the **Catalog button.**

10.   Click on the **Start Compare button** to begin the comparison process.

PROGRAM LEVELS

The same three program levels are available as in the Backup window—Preset, Basic, and Advanced, and these are set in the Configure window. Each higher step provides increased control over the details of the way Norton Backup for Windows works.

● OPTIONS–PRESET

Backup Set Catalog   This box has the name and description of the master catalogs created when backup sets were made. Choose the backup set you want to compare.

Select Files   This button opens the Select Compare Files window where you can select the files to compare.

Compare From   This box allows you to choose the location of the backed up files.

● OPTIONS–BASIC

The Basic and Advanced comparison options are very similar; the only difference is found in the options for selecting files. At the Basic program level, the options include all the options at the Preset level, plus the following:

Backup Set Catalog   This lets you choose from individual catalogs or from the master catalog from each backup set.

Compare To   This lets you select the location from where to compare the backup set. The choices are the following:

- Original Locations
- Alternate Drives
- Alternate Directories
- Single Directory

Options   The Options button lets you choose to toggle two additional options:

- Audible Prompts (Beep)
- Quit After Compare

Catalog   The Catalog button allows you to locate a catalog stored in another drive or directory, or to rebuild or retrieve one from the backup diskettes. The options are the following:

- **Load** to load a different catalog file from a different directory.

- **Retrieve** to get a catalog file stored on the last disk of a backup set.

- **Rebuild** to rebuild a catalog file by scanning the diskettes in a backup set.

- **Delete** to delete a catalog file.

● OPTIONS–ADVANCED

The Advanced program level options are the same as in the Basic program level options, except that in the Select Compare Files window, you can select files using the *Special* button to include files based on a range of dates, and to exclude them based on file type (copy protected, read-only, system, or hidden).

Selecting Files

Selecting files in the Select Compare Files window is very similar to selecting files in the Select Backup Files window. There are, however, two major differences. The first is that there is no View option available to view a file. The other is that at the Advanced program level, the Include and Exclude buttons are missing, only the Special button appears.

THE RESTORE WINDOW

Backing up files is fine, and it is a good idea to compare the backed up files to the originals, but ultimately the reason for backing up files is so that you can, in the event of disaster, restore them. The restoration process is very similar to the comparison process, and many of the options are the same. The main difference is that with Restore you are actually writing the files to your hard disk, not merely comparing them.

To Restore Files

1. Click on the **Configure button** to open the Configure window.

2. Select the program level to use.

3. Click on the **Restore button** to switch to the Restore window.

4. Select the backup catalog to use.

5. Select the files to restore by clicking on the **Select Files button** and selecting the files in the Select Restore Files window.

6. Select the drive to restore from.

7. If using the Basic or Advanced program level, select the location of the files you want to restore to.

8. If using the Basic or Advanced program level, click on the **Options button** to set the options desired.

9. If using the Basic or Advanced program level, and you want to use a catalog not on the default drive and directory, or you need to rebuild a catalog, click on the **Catalog button.**

10. Click on the **Start Restore button** to begin the restore process.

PROGRAM LEVELS

The same three program levels are available as in the Backup window—Preset, Basic, and Advanced, and these are set in the Configure window.

● OPTIONS–PRESET

Backup Set Catalog   This box has the name and description of the master catalogs that were created when the backup sets were made. Choose the backup set you want to restore.

Select Files   This button opens the Select Restore Files window where you can select the files to restore.

Restore From   This box lets you choose the location from which the backed up files are restored.

● OPTIONS–BASIC

The Basic and Advanced restore options are very similar; the only difference is in the options available for selecting files. At the Basic program level, the options include all the options at the Preset level, plus the following:

Backup Set Catalog   This now lets you choose from individual catalogs or from the master catalog for each backup set.

Restore To   This lets you select the location to which to restore the backup set. The choices are the following:

- Original Location
- Alternate Drives
- Alternate Directories
- Single Directory

Options   The Options button lets you choose to toggle several additional options. These are the following:

- **Verify Restored Files** When on, Norton Backup for Windows compares the file on the backup disk and the file written to the hard disk. This slows the backup process, but greatly improves the confidence level.

- **Prompt Before Creating Directories**   When on, Norton Backup for Windows will ask for verification before it creates a directory.

- **Prompt Before Creating Files**   When on, Norton Backup for Windows will ask for verification before it creates a new file that doesn't already exist on the hard disk.

- **Prompt Before Overwriting Existing Files**   When on, Norton Backup for Windows will ask for verification before it overwrites an existing file.

- **Restore Empty Directories**   When on, Norton Backup for Windows will create directories that do not exist on the hard disk, even if there are no files to restore from that directory.

- **Audible Prompts (Beep)**   When on, Norton Backup for Windows will beep whenever an action is required on your part, or an error condition occurs. Note that this beep will not occur if you have "Beep=no" in your WIN.INI file.

- **Quit After Restore**   When on, Norton Backup for Windows will automatically quit when the restoration is completed.

Catalog   The Catalog button lets you locate a catalog stored in another drive or directory, or rebuild one from the backup diskettes. The options are the following:

- **Load** to load a different catalog file.

- **Retrieve** to get a catalog file stored on the last disk of a backup set.

- **Rebuild** to rebuild a catalog file by scanning the diskettes in a backup set.

- **Delete** to delete a catalog file.

● OPTIONS–ADVANCED

The Advanced program level options are similar to the Basic program level options, except that in the Select Restore Files window, you can select files using the *Special* button to include files based on a range of dates, and to exclude them based on file type (copy protected, read-only, system, or hidden), and in the following options which are available by clicking on the **Options** button:

Data Verification   Three choices are provided for data verification. They are the following:

- **Read and Compare** which checks every byte.
- **Sample Only** which checks every eighth track.
- **Off** which does no checking.

Overwrite Files   Three levels of overwrite protection are available. They are the following:

- **Never Overwrite** tells Norton Backup for Windows not to restore a file if it already exists on the hard disk.
- **Older Files Only** tells Norton Backup for Windows to restore a file to the hard disk only if the file on the hard disk is older than the file being restored.
- **Always Overwrite** tells Norton Backup for Windows to always overwrite an existing file on the hard disk, regardless of the age of the file.

Archive Flag   Three different actions are available for the archive flag. They are the following:

- **Leave alone** instructs Norton Backup for Windows not to change the status of the archive flag when it restores the file.
- **Mark as backed up** causes Norton Backup for Windows to set the archive flag off for all restored files.
- **Mark as NOT backed up** causes Norton Backup for Windows to set the archive flag on for all restored files.

Selecting Files

Selecting files in the Select Restore Files window is the same process as selecting files in the Select Compare Files window.

USING AUTOMATED BACKUPS

Norton Backup for Windows provides tools for creating and using automated backups to make the process as simple and as fast as possible. Automated backups can be created only at the Basic or Advanced program level, but they can be used at any program level. You can also use the Scheduler to begin your backup automatically, and run it in the background.

SETUP FILES

Setup files contain all that is necessary to automate a backup because they include the type of backup, the file selection, backup options, and restore and compare selections and options. When you create a backup at the Advanced or Basic level, all the commands and options that you select at that level will apply even if the setup file is used at another level. You can tell Norton Backup for Windows to use a setup file on start up by including the name of the setup file in the command line. If you want the backup to start automatically, include a /**A** (for automatic) on the command line as well.

● EXAMPLE

To start Norton Backup for Windows, using a setup file that includes all your Quattro Pro worksheet files, select **Run** from the Norton Desktop for Windows File menu, and key in the following command line:

```
NBWIN.EXE QPRO.SET /A
```

MACROS

Norton Backup for Windows includes a macro recorder that will record your keystrokes. You can use this, along with your setup

files, to automate a complicated set of backup commands or to provide other users with the ability to select certain files while still
giving them a more limited set of options.

Macros are stored with the current setup file, and only one macro
can be stored with each setup file. You can record another macro even
though you may have one already stored with the current setup file,
but only the most recent one will be used and saved. Macros should be
recorded at the level they will be used, and must begin while in the
Backup window, though they can be used to automate restore and
compare operations as well.

If you intend to use a macro at the Preset program level, you must
begin it at that level. Because there is no menu option for macros at
the Preset level, you will need to use the function keys to begin,
end, or insert pauses in the macro. To begin recording the macro,
press **F7**. To insert a pause in the macro to allow the user to select
files, press **F9**. The recording will pause until you leave the current
window or dialog box, and then will begin recording again. To end
the macro, press **F7**.

At the Basic or Advanced program level, you can begin macros by
selecting **Record** from the Macro menu, or by pressing **F7**. To play
back a macro, you must also start at the Backup window, then press
F8, or select **Run** from the Macro menu.

You can also automatically start the macro associated with a setup
file from the command line by including an @ sign in front of the
setup filename on the command line.

● EXAMPLE

To automatically start the macro you created to go with your Quattro Pro setup file, you would use the following command line:

NBWIN.EXE @QPRO.SET

Command Line

You can use command line options to start Norton Backup for Windows automatically, run a specific macro and setup file, and select

the type of backup. Norton Backup for Windows supports the following command line options:

@   Runs macro associated with the setup file.

/A   Immediately starts the backup.

/M   Runs Norton Backup for Windows mimimized.

/TF   Does a Full Backup.

/TI   Does an Incremental backup.

/TD   Does a Differential backup.

/TC   Does a Full copy backup.

/TO   Does an Incremental copy backup.

Note that the @ and /A command line options are mutually exclusive, and that the @ option overrides the /A option.

Part Six

Configuring the Desktop

BUTTON BAR

The Button bar at the bottom of the Drive Windows can be omitted by deselecting the Display Button Bar box in the Configure Button Bar window, or it can be edited in various ways.

By default, the buttons that appear on the Button bar are the following:

- Move
- Copy
- Delete
- View Pane
- Type Sort
- Name Sort

To Change the Button Command

1. Select **Button Bar**... from the Configure menu.

2. Find the command you want on the Menu Item list and select it using the mouse.

3. Click the **button** to which you want the command assigned.

4. Select **OK** when you are finished. To make the change permanent, use **Save Configuration** from the Configure menu or the **Save Configuration on Exit** checkbox in the Configure Preferences menu.

● NOTE   Select commands carefully. For example, the Menu Item list includes two items named "All." One is from the Select menu and the other from the Deselect menu. Even though their names are the same, their functions are exactly opposite.

To Edit the Text on Buttons

1. Select the **Edit button** in the Configure Button Bar dialog box.

2. In the Edit Button Bar dialog box, click on the **text box** of the button you want to modify and key in the text. The program will beep if you attempt to enter too much text.

3. Click on **OK** when you are finished.

● **NOTE** Take care not to change the meaning of the button. Changing the text on the button changes only its appearance. The function of the button can be changed only by selecting another Menu Item in the Configure Button Bar window.

CONFIRMATION REQUESTS

You can take many actions in Norton Desktop for Windows—some of which you may later regret. To protect yourself from various types of hasty actions, you can toggle on dialog boxes that will ask for confirmation of the action to be taken.

To Be Prompted for Filenames

1. Select **Preferences** from the Configure menu.

2. From the Prompt for Filename box, choose the operations for which you would like a prompt.

3. Click on **OK** when you are finished.

● **NOTE** The Prompt for Filename option works when you first select one or more files from a Drive Window and then choose the Edit, View, Print, or Delete functions. It is a precaution that allows you to change your mind before taking an action. If you don't want to be prompted, clear some or all of the check boxes.

To Select Confirmation Requests

You can choose to have dialog boxes pop up and ask for confirmation when certain potentially "dangerous" operations are attempted. To do this, follow these steps:

1.   Select **Confirmation** from the Configure menu.

2.   Click on the **confirmation** options you want.

3.   Click on **OK** when you are finished.

• OPTIONS

Delete   Warning appears when you are deleting an unprotected file. If Erase Protect is on, the warning message will not appear, but you will still be asked to confirm the deletion.

Subtree Delete   Warning appears for any operation involving the removal of a directory.

Replace   Warning appears for any copy operation that involves overwriting another file. This box should *remain checked* because if you write over a file, the file will be lost and will not be recoverable by any means.

Mouse Operation   Opens a confirmation dialog box for all mouse operations that move, copy, or delete files.

Unformatted Print   Warning appears when you try to print a file for which there is no associated application. This will appear whether the Print File command from the File menu is used or the file has been dragged from a Drive Window to the Desktop Printer Icon.

CONTROL MENUS

Control menus are menus that appear when you click once on a desktop icon or when you click once on the control box in the upper left corner of application windows. The application window's Control menu can be configured. The desktop icon's menu can only be turned on or off.

To Configure the Control Box Menus

1. Choose Preferences… from the Configure menu.

2. The Control Menu check boxes are in the lower left corner of the Configure Preferences dialog box. Select any of the items you want to appear on the menus. Click on **OK** when you are finished. Then, your selections will be available from the control box on any application window.

To Turn on the Drive/Tool Icon Control Menu

1. Select **Preferences**… from the Configure menu.

2. Click on the **Drive/Tool Icon Control Menu** check box.

3. Click on **OK** when you are finished.

● MENU OPTIONS

Click once on a drive icon or desktop icon to see the Control menu.

Open   Opens the drive or starts the program.

Icon   Allows you to select another icon.

Label   Opens a dialog box where you can change the label that appears under the icon.

Close   Closes the drive or program and removes the icon from the desktop.

DESKTOP ICONS

Icons on the desktop represent either a program or a file with its associated program. The appearance of icons can be changed by selecting from the icons available in the Norton Desktop for Windows, or by designing your own icons using the Icon Editor.

To Select Tool Icons

1. Choose **Preferences** from the Configure menu.
2. In the Tool Icons box, check the boxes for the icons you want on the desktop when Norton Desktop for Windows starts. If you have more than one printer, click on the **Printers**... button to choose the printer that you want associated with the Printer Icon. Up to four printers, including a fax machine, can be selected, and each printer will have its own icon.
3. When you have made your selections, click on **OK**.

● **NOTE**   To reduce desktop clutter, you do not have to create an icon for every printer that you might want to use. The full Printer Selection box is also available when you select Print from the File menu.

To Change Icon Label

1. Click once on the **desktop icon**.
2. Choose **Label**... from the pop-up menu.
3. Key in the **label** you want to appear on the icon.
4. Select **OK** when you are finished.

● **NOTE**   The Drive/Tool Icon Control Menu option must be switched on to change the icon or the icon label. This check box item is available under Preferences in the Configure menu.

To Change a Desktop Icon

1. Click once on the **desktop icon**.
2. Select **Icon**... from the pop-up menu.

3. The Choose Icon dialog box opens as shown in Figure VI.1. The Icon File text box shows the path for the current icon. Click on the **prompt button** to see a list of the filenames and paths of your most recent choices. The Icon(s) box shows the current icon. Click on the Icons **prompt button** to see all the icons available in the current path.

4. Choose an **icon** from the **Icon(s) box**. If the icon you want is not in the currently selected path, click on the **Browse button**.

5. Highlight the **source file** you want and click on **OK**. To see the icons in the source file, select the **View button** in the Choose Icon dialog box.

6. Scroll up and down the Icon(s) box to find the icon you want. Highlight the **icon** and click on **OK**. The highlighted icon will be transferred to the Desktop icon automatically.

● **NOTE** The source files for icons will have one of four extensions: .ICO, .NIL, .EXE or .DLL. Therefore, the Browse box will show only those files with these extensions. However, not all files with

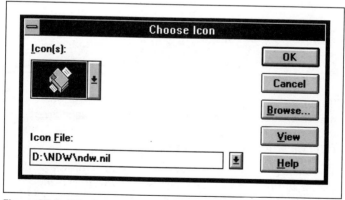

Figure VI.1: The Choose Icon dialog box

these extensions will have icons in them. If you select a new source file, click the **View button** and if the icon does not change, it means that the selected file contains no icons.

EDITOR

Any Editor program can be used to edit files in response to the Edit command on the File menu. The default editor is Notepad.

To Set a New Default Editor

1. Select **Editor**... from the Configure menu.

2. Key in the full path of the editor program that you want to use. If you don't know the exact name of the program, click on the **Browse button**. Highlight the **name** of the editor and then select **OK**. The editor name will be returned to the Editor Program text box. Then select **OK** again to save the new default editor.

MENUS

By default, the Norton Desktop menu bar starts with short menus that contain only the most commonly used commands. All commands are listed in the full menus, which are reached by choosing Full Menus from the Configure menu.

The menus and the menu bar are not static. You can add new menus and redesign existing menus in any way that suits you. If you specify a password, only users who know it will be able to get to the full custom menus.

When you select Edit Custom Menus... from the Configure menu, you will see the Menu Assignments dialog box as shown in Figure VI.2.

To Add a Function to an Existing Menu

1. Choose **Edit Custom Menus**... from the Configure menu.

2. Scroll through the Command list and highlight the **command** you want. When you pick an item, a brief description of its function will appear in the lower left corner of the dialog box.

3. In the Menu List box, highlight the **item** that you want to directly follow the new function.

4. Click on the **Add button** and the new command will be inserted right above the highlighted menu item. Click on **OK**.

● **NOTE**   If you do not highlight a menu item, the Add function will not work.

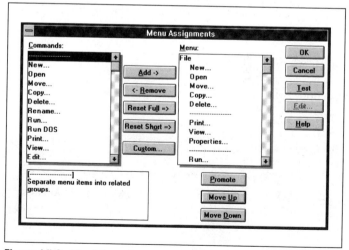

Figure VI.2: The Menu Assignments dialog box

To Delete a Menu Item

1. Select **Edit Custom Menus**… from the Configure menu.

2. Highlight the **item** you want to delete in the Menu box.

3. Click on **Remove**. The item will be deleted. Click on **OK** to exit the dialog box.

To Make a Custom Menu

1. Select **Edit Custom Menus**… from the Configure menu.

2. Click on the **Custom button** in the Menu Assignments dialog box.

3. In the Type of item box, click on the **radio button** for New Menu.

4. Key in the title for the menu in the Text box. Click on **OK** when you are finished.

5. To preview the results, click the **Test button** in the Menu Assignments box to see what the new menu will look like. The title will appear as the leftmost menu in the menu bar. Use the Control box menu to close the menu Test window.

6. Click the **OK** button when you are finished.

● **NOTE**   To include an Alt-key accelerator in the menu name, key in an ampersand directly in front of the accelerator letter. For example, key in **&Sales** and the menu will be highlighted when you enter the Alt-S key combination.

To Create a Custom Menu Item

1. Select **Edit Custom Menus**… from the Configure menu.

2. Click on the **Custom button** in the Menu Assignments dialog box.

3. Under Type of item, click on the **radio button** for New Command.

4. In the Text box, key in the **name** of the item as you want it to appear in the menu.

5. Key in the **name** of the program, or script, or file that you want to launch when this menu item is selected. The Command line must either be the complete path for the program to be launched or a filename with an associated extension.

6. If you want a shortcut key, enter the key or key combination in the Shortcut Key text box. Click on the **check box** if you want the shortcut key to display in the menu listing.

7. Click on **OK**. Preview the menu by clicking on the **Test button**. Select **OK** again when you are finished.

• **NOTE**   Shortcut keys are very handy for getting to a menu item quickly. See Shortcut Keys later in Part VI for the rules that govern the key combinations available for shortcut keys.

To Edit a Standard Menu Item

1. Select **Edit Custom Menus**... from the Configure menu. The Menu Assignments dialog box will open.

2. Highlight the Menu item you wish to edit and click on the **Edit button** to open the Edit Menu Text Item dialog box.

3. In the Text box, key in the **name** as you want it to appear on the menu. Include an ampersand directly in front of the letter that you want underlined.

4. Key in a **shortcut key**, if you want one, and click on the **check box** if you want the shortcut key to show in the menu.

5. The original setting for the item is shown at the top of the dialog box. Click on the **Original button** if you want to restore it. Select **OK** when you are finished.

To Edit a Customized Menu Item

1. Select **Edit Custom Menus**... from the Configure menu.

2. In the Menu Assignments dialog box, highlight the custom menu item you want to edit, then click on the **Edit button**. The Edit Customized Menu Item dialog box will open.

3. Edit the menu item. Click on **OK** when finished or **Cancel** to abandon the operation.

To Change the Order of Menu Items

1. Open the Menu Assignments dialog box by selecting **Edit Custom Menus**... from the Configure menu.

2. Using the scroll bar on the Menu box, highlight the item that you want to move.

   - To move the item up one position, click on the **Move Up button**.
   - To move the item down one position, click on the **Move Down button**.
   - To promote an item up though the menu hierarchy, highlight it and click on the **Promote button**. To demote the item, click on the **Move Down button**.

3. Use the **Test button** to view the menu you have constructed. Close the Menu Test box. Click on **OK** when you are finished.

● **NOTE**   Items can also be moved up and down by clicking on them and then dragging them to the position you want.

Names that are flush left in the Menu list are menu bar items. Indented under these are items directly under a menu title. The next indentation is for items in a cascaded menu.

To Remove a Menu or Menu Item

1. Select **Edit Custom Menus**... from the Configure menu.

2. In the Menu box, highlight the **item** you want to remove.

3. Click on the **Remove** button. If you pick a single command, it will be deleted without further warning. If you choose a menu, a warning box will open advising you that the menu and all the items below it will be deleted if you proceed. Make your choice and click on **OK** when the deletion is finished.

To Restore Original Menus

If you decide either to rebuild your custom menus or to abandon them completely, you can easily reset the Short or Full Menus to their original configurations.

1.   Select **Edit Custom Menus**... from the Configure menu.

2.   To reset the menu to the default Full Menus, choose **Reset Full**. To reset to Short Menus, choose **Reset Short**.

3.   Click on **OK** when you are finished.

PASSWORDS

If a password dialog box appears, it means that you have entered an area where a password is required. Passwords can be maintained for three different areas:

- **Custom menus:** Passwords can be set to prevent users from accessing certain menu commands. This type of password is set using **Password**... in the Configure menu.

- **Quick Access:** Passwords can restrict the use of groups or objects in Quick Access. (See *Changing Objects,* Part III, "Running Quick Access.")

- **Sleeper:** A password can be specified to unlock the screen and keyboard when Sleeper is activated. (See *Sleeper,* Part IV, "Tools and Utilities.")

To Set a Menu Password

1.   Select **Password**... from the Configure menu.

2.   Key in the password that you want in the Password text box. The password, which can be up to 20 characters long, appears as asterisks to ensure privacy.

3.   Press **OK** and a Confirm Password box will appear. Key in the password a second time and choose **OK** again.

144   Configuring the Desktop

Note that once a password has been set and you switch to Short Menus under the Configure menu, you will need the password to return to Full Menus.

● **NOTE**   To make the password permanent, you must choose **Save Configuration** from the Configure menu or check the **Save Configuration on Exit** check box in the Preferences… dialog box under the Configure menu. Otherwise, the password is in effect only for this session of Norton Desktop for Windows.

To Remove a Menu Password

1. Select **Password**… from the Configure menu.

2. You will be asked first for the current password. Key it in the Password text box and choose **OK**.

3. In the Enter New Password dialog box, key in the **new password** and click on **OK**. If you want no password, press the **Enter** key.

4. The next box will ask you to confirm the password or to confirm that you don't want a password. Either key in the new password and click on **OK**, or press **Enter** to confirm that you want no password.

SAVING THE CONFIGURATION

Changes in Edit Custom Menus, Shortcut Keys, SmartErase, and Launch List will be saved automatically, but you must use one of the save methods for other changes to be made permanently. The two methods have some overlapping functions, but they are not identical.

To Save the Appearance of Your Desktop

This method will preserve the appearance of your desktop as you leave it.

1. Select **Preferences**... from the Configure menu.

2. Check the **Save Configuration on Exit** box.

3. Click on **OK** when you are finished. When you next start Norton Desktop for Windows, the desktop will be as it was when you left it.

To Restart with a Standard Desktop

Arrange the desktop the way you want it to appear when you next start Norton Desktop for Windows. Click on **Save Configuration** from the Configure menu. Note that the desktop will continue to reopen with this appearance until the next time you click on Save Configuration.

SHORTCUT KEYS

With shortcut keys you can choose menu commands without opening a menu. Setting the shortcut keys for your commonly used functions can save you time and keystrokes.

To Assign a Shortcut Key

1. Select **Shortcut Keys**... from the Configure menu. The Configure Shortcut Keys dialog box opens as shown in Figure VI.3.

2. All the commands available in the default Full Menus are in the Menu Item box. Scroll though the box until you find the command you want. Highlight the command.

3. In the New Key text box, key in the shortcut key that you want assigned to this command. Use the actual keystrokes.

If you use an invalid key combination, the keyboard will refuse it.

4.   If you want the shortcut key to appear in the menu next to the command, check the box next to the Include key name in standard menu.

5.   Click on **OK** when you are finished.

These are the keys you can use for shortcut keys:

- Any function key except F1 (F1 reserved for Help);

- Any combination of the Shift key plus a function key (except F1);

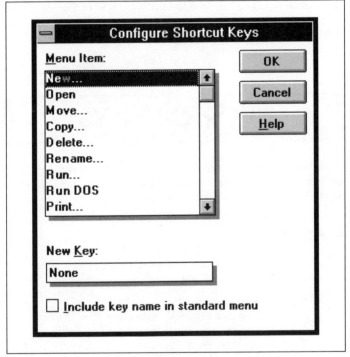

Figure VI.3: The Configure Shortcut Keys dialog box

- A combination of the Ctrl key and any function key, number, letter, or direction key;

- A combination of the Ctrl and Shift key and any function key, number, letter, or direction key;

- A combination of the Alt key with either the Shift or Ctrl key plus a function key, number, letter, or direction key.

● **NOTE**   You can use the numbers at the top of the keyboard and the numbers on the numeric keypad as different numbers. For example, Ctrl-8 using the number 8 from the regular keyboard is a completely different shortcut key from Ctrl-8 using the numeric keypad 8.

● **WARNING**   Shortcut keys can also be assigned using the Launch Manager. If you reuse a shortcut key, the one assigned by the Launch Manager takes precedence.

Appendix A

Installation

To install Norton Desktop for Windows, you will need the following hardware and software:

- IBM AT, PS/2 (286 and up) or a 100-percent compatible clone.

- A hard disk drive with at least 5.6 Mb of free space.

  1 Mb or more of RAM (3 Mb is recommended).

- Windows 3.0 or higher.

- MS-DOS or PC-DOS, 3.1 or higher.

- Any monitor that can display Windows 3.0 or higher.

A Microsoft mouse or a 100-percent compatible mouse is also recommended.

To Install Norton Desktop for Windows from DOS

1. Insert Disk No. 1 in the appropriate floppy drive.

2. Key in

  a:install

  If the disk is in drive b:, substitute **b:**.

3. Follow the instructions on the screen.

To Install Norton Desktop for Windows from Inside Windows

1. Start Windows. Insert Disk No. 1 in the appropriate floppy drive.

2. Pull down the File menu in Program Manager and select **Run**....

3. In the Command Line text box, key in

a:install

or

b:install

depending on where you inserted the diskette and click on **OK** or press **Enter**.

4. Follow the instructions on the screen.

To Do a Complete Installation

After following one of the procedures above, you can begin the installation.

1. First, you will be prompted to key in both your name and your company's name in order to proceed. An entry must be made in both text boxes. Click on **OK**. The program will then search for a previously installed version of Norton Desktop for Windows.

2. The Install Norton Desktop Files To... box will open. The program will insert C:\NDW as the default drive and directory for installation in the Install To text box. The Target Drive Status box shows the space available on the drive before and after installation. To change drives, click on your choice in the Drives box. The Target Drive Status information will change to reflect the space available on the new drive.

3. If you do *not* want to install all of the components of Norton Desktop for Windows, click on the Select button. The Application Selection box will open. Click on the programs you do **not** want to install in order to deselect them. Select the **OK** button when you are finished. The Install Norton Desktop Files To... window will change to show the number of applications selected, the amount of hard disk space required, and the available space on the selected drive. When you are satisfied with your choices,

click on **OK** in the Install Norton Desktop Files To...
dialog box.

4. Installation of the files will begin. You will be prompted
for additional program diskettes as they are needed.

5. The program will open the Modify AUTOEXEC.BAT file
dialog box to inform you that the programs requested require changes to your AUTOEXEC.BAT file. You can
choose from one of the following options:

- **Let Install modify the AUTOEXEC.BAT file**. This
  option will allow the install program to make the
  necessary changes to the AUTOEXEC.BAT file automatically. To examine or modify the changes, select
  the **Edit button**. The box will enlarge to include a
  screen showing your current AUTOEXEC.BAT file
  with the changes included. Make any edits you
  want and click on **OK** when you are finished.

- **Save the required changes to new file**. If you select
  this option, the AUTOEXEC.BAT file, as modified by
  the Install program, will be saved under the name
  AUTOEXEC.NEW. Your current AUTOEXEC.BAT file
  will not be modified in any way. Later, if you choose,
  you can rename the AUTOEXEC.NEW file to
  AUTOEXEC.BAT, if you decide to adopt the changes.

- **Do not make any changes**. No changes will be made to
  your AUTOEXEC.BAT file if you choose this option.
  Note that some Norton Desktop for Windows
  programs may **not** function properly, or at all, without
  modifications to the AUTOEXEC.BAT file.

6. A dialog box will ask if you want to schedule an automatic
backup of files. If you select Yes, the automatic backup will
be placed in the Scheduler. You will, however, still have to
configure Norton Backup to perform the scheduled backup
of files. If you select No, the automatic backup will be listed
in the Scheduler's list of events, but it will not be enabled.

7. The Norton Desktop group window opens. Icons for the
programs you have chosen to install will appear inside the
window. Next you will be asked if you want to install the

Norton Desktop as your Windows shell in place of the Program Manager. If you select Yes, the install program will make the necessary changes automatically in the SYSTEM.INI file. Using Norton Desktop as your shell will save Windows memory. Note that the Program Manager files are neither deleted nor changed, but they are removed from view. If you select No, minimize the Program Manager while you are running Norton Desktop.

8. At the completion of installation, the program will open an Install Complete dialog box as well as a Notepad window containing a README.TXT file. This file has information not included in the documentation. Click on the Notepad window to read the file. After you read the file, close the text window. You will be able to read it again by selecting it from the Norton Desktop directory.

9. If changes were made to your AUTOEXEC.BAT file, choose Reboot from the Installation Complete window. If no changes were made, select Restart Windows.

● **NOTE**   If you do not install all the Norton Desktop programs and wish to add them later, you can run the Install program again. At that time select only the additional programs from the Application Selection dialog box.

Appendix B

The Norton Windows Batch Language

When operating under DOS, a batch file makes it easier to do everyday operations. It is a simple ASCII text file that has each command on a separate line. Batch files perform a series of commands automatically.

The Norton Windows Batch Language provides this same capability, and much more, for the Windows environment. Windows Batch Language files are simple ASCII text files that contain the commands to perform your Windows operations automatically. They can be edited with any editor or word processor that can produce ASCII output, or with Batch Builder. Batch Builder has the added advantage of having a built-in, handy on-line reference to the Windows Batch Language commands. Windows Batch Language can help you to create interactive, intelligent scripts to automate many ordinary tasks in Windows.

Abs(integer)   Returns the positive (absolute) value of an integer. **Example:**

   delta = Abs(i–j)

AskLine(title,prompt,default)   Requests a line of data from the user. The entire response is returned if the user clicks on **OK** or presses **Enter**. A **Cancel** aborts processing of the batch file. **Example:**

   User = AskLine("UserName",
   "Please Enter Your Name:", "")

AskYesNo(title,question)   Requests a Yes, No, or Cancel response from the user, returning @YES or @NO. A **Cancel** aborts processing of the batch file. **Example:**

   rep = AskYesNo("BackupTime?", "ready to backup your work?")

Average(integer(, integer)…)   Yields the integer average of a series of integers, separated by commas. Because the result is an integer, substantial rounding error is possible. **Example:**

> **AvgAge = Average(Tom_Age, Dick_Age, Harry_Age)**
>
> **Message("The average age of Tom, Dick and Harry is: ", AvgAge)**

Beep   Produces a single, short beep. This beep will not be heard, however, if your WIN.INI file contains the line "Beep=no". **Example:**

> **Beep**
>
> **AskYesNo("DATA ALERT!!!", "This could permanently destroy data. Are you SURE you want to proceed?")**

Call(filename.wbt,parameters)   Passes control to another WBT file temporarily. It can also pass parameters to the secondary WBT file. All variables are global to both the main WBT file and the secondary one, and can be modified by the secondary WBT file. Multiple parameters are separated by spaces. If parameters are passed, they will automatically be converted to "param1", "param2", and so forth. The variable "param0" will contain the number of parameters passed. The secondary file should end with a Return statement to pass control back to the main file. **Example:**

> **Call("qprobak.wbt", "*.wq1 *.wq!")**

CallExt(filename.wbt,parameters)   Calls a secondary WBT file in a similar fashion to Call, except that although all variables with Call are global and thus can be modified by the secondary batch file, all variables with CallExt are local to each file. Parameters, however, can be passed to the secondary file. If multiple parameters are passed, they will be converted to "param1", "param2", and so forth, automatically. The variable "param0" will contain the number of parameters passed. A Return statement is required at the end of the secondary file to return control to the calling file. **Example:**

> **CallExt("savefile.wbt",currentfile)**

Char2Num(string)   Takes a text string and converts its first character to its ANSI code equivalent. The returned value is an integer. **Example:**

> strvar = "Alex"
>
> ansi = Char2Num(strvar)
>
> Message("ANSI Eq", "The ANSI equivalent of the first character in %strvar% is: %ansi%")

ClipAppend(string)   Adds a string to the Windows Clipboard after the current contents. The clipboard must either be empty or contain only text data, or an error message will be returned. If the append is successful, the function returns @TRUE, if it is unsuccessful, it returns @FALSE. **Example:**

> response = AskLine("UserName",
> "What is your name?", "")
>
> ClipAppend(response)

ClipGet( )   Gets the current contents of the Windows Clipboard, and returns it as a single string. The clipboard should contain only text. **Example:**

> ;The following will get the user's name, convert it
>
> ;to uppercase, and store it in the variable "Name".
>
> response = AskLine("UserName",
> "What is your name?", "")
>
> ClipPut(StrUpper(response))
>
> Name = ClipGet()

ClipPut(string)   Copies a string to the Windows Clipboard, where, unlike ClipAppend, it replaces the current contents of the clipboard.

DateTime( )   Returns the date and time of the system as a formatted string. The format may be altered by changing the international section of the WIN.INI file. This can be changed either by editing it directly, or using the International section of the Control Panel. **Example:**

> Message("The current date and time are: ", DateTime())

Debug(@ON ┆ @OFF)   Toggles debug mode on or off. When debug mode is @ON, WinBatch will step through the WBT file, displaying a dialog box with the statement just executed, any results from that statement, the errors from that step, and the next statement to execute. When debug mode is @OFF, the default, batch files execute normally. **Example:**

```
;This next runs the batch file step by step
Debug(@ON)
```

Delay(seconds)   Inserts a pause in the batch file of from 2–15 seconds. **Example:**

```
Message("!!WAIT!!", "Please be patient, this may take a
while")
Delay(5)
Message("Done", "OK, that is done now.")
```

DialogBox("title", "filename.wbd")   Pops up a Windows dialog box. The contents and appearance of this dialog box are controlled by a template file. This template file must have the extension .WBD.

Each item in a WBD file is enclosed in brackets ([ ]) and contains a variable plus one of the following symbols:

Symbol	Meaning
+	check box
#	text box
\	file selection list box
^	option button
$	Variable

The check box and option button symbols each require a number which represents a value that gets assigned to the variable when the box or button is selected. Following the number is the text that will appear beside the button or box. Anything not within square brackets is displayed as text. The first item that appears in a group of option buttons will always be the default. Note that template files are limited to 15 lines and the first 60 columns, and must contain no tab characters. **Example:**

DialogBox("Edit a File", "ed_diag.wbd")

DirChange((d:)path)   Changes to a new directory and optionally to a new drive. Returns @TRUE if the change was successful, @FALSE if not. **Example:**

DirChange("c:\")
TextBox("The contents of your autoexec.bat file",
"autoexec.bat")

DirGet( )   Returns a string whose value is the path of the current directory. Useful when you want to change directories temporarily, but be sure to return to the original directory when finished. **Example:**

startpoint = DirGet()
DirChange("c:\")
TextBox("The contents of your autoexec.bat file are:",
"autoexec.bat")
DirChange(startpoint)

DirHome( )   Returns a string whose value is the drive and directory of the WINBATCH.EXE file. **Example:**

homedir = DirHome()
Message("The WinBatch executable files are in
",homedir)

DirItemize(dirlist)   Returns a list of directories, separated by spaces. Used with ItemSelect which requires a list separated by spaces. Accepts wildcards in its arguments. **Example:**

diravail = DirItemize("*")

DirMake((d:)path)   Makes a new subdirectory. Returns @TRUE if successful, @FALSE if not. **Example:**

DirMake("\winstuff")

DirRemove(dirlist)   Deletes one or more directories. Accepts a list of directories separated by spaces. Does not allow wildcards. Returns @TRUE if successful, @FALSE if not. **Example:**

   DirRemove("temp" "junk" "\garbage")

DirRename((d:)oldpath, (d:)newpath)   Changes the name of a directory. Returns @TRUE if successful, @FALSE if not. **Example:**

   DirRename("\ndwtemp", "\ndwicons")

DiskFree(drivelist)   Returns the total of free disk space on one or more drives. Accepts a list of drives, separated by spaces. Ignores all except the first character of each item in the list, so it treats "c:\ d:\win" exactly the same as "c d". **Example:**

   dfree = DiskFree("d")
   Message("D: Drive", "There are %dfree% bytes of space free on D:")

Display(seconds, window title, message)   Displays a text message box for 1–15 seconds. Unlike Pause, Display may be canceled with any keystroke or mouse click. **Example:**

   Display(5,"Coffee Time", "Please be patient, this may take a while")

DOSVersion(@MAJOR ¦ @MINOR)   Returns the current DOS version number, either the major or minor revision number. **Example:**

   main = DOSVersion(@MAJOR)
   rev = DOSVersion(@MINOR)
   Display(5,"DOS Revision", "This computer is using DOS Version %main%.%rev%.")

Drop(var (, var) …)   Eliminates a variable and its name, and frees up the memory associated with it. **Example:**

   foo = "A silly long string that takes up a lot of space and memory, but doesn't do anything useful."
   Drop(foo) ; Frees up the memory and space used by foo.

EndSession( )   This quits Windows and exits to DOS. It will save any configuration changes you may have made *if* NDW.INI has SAVE=TRUE in its configuration section. If not, any changes will be abandoned. **Example:**

> **done = AskYesNo ("End Session?", "Are you sure you want to Quit?")**
>
> **If done == @YES Then Goto quit**
>
> **Display(3,"", "End Session Aborted")**
>
> **Exit**
>
> **:quit**
>
> **EndSession()**

Environment(variable)   Queries the DOS environment for a specific variable and returns the value of that variable as a string. **Example:**

> **dosprompt = Environment("PROMPT")**
>
> **Display(3,"Prompt", "The current DOS Prompt is: %dosprompt%")**

ErrorMode(@CANCEL ¦ @NOTIFY ¦ @OFF)   Modifies the effect of an error in a batch file. The default is @CANCEL which cancels the execution of the batch file. @NOTIFY causes the error to be reported to the user, who can choose to continue if the error is not a fatal one. @OFF causes minor errors to be suppressed. Moderate to fatal errors are reported to the user, who can elect to continue if it isn't a fatal error. Returns the previous mode. **Example:**

> **; The Following will delete the file "temp.jnk" from the**
>
> **; c:\garbage directory, if it exists, but if it doesn't, it**
>
> **; will not cause an error message, but will continue to the**
>
> **; next line of the batch file.**
>
> **prevmode = ErrorMode(@OFF)**
>
> **FileDelete ("c:\garbage\temp.jnk")**
>
> **ErrorMode(prevmode)**

Exclusive(@OFF ¦ @ON)   This is a toggle that determines whether other Windows programs get a share of the processing time.

Defaults to @OFF, which doesn't interfere with other programs, but will tend to run somewhat slower if there are several windows open. When set to @ON it will prevent other Windows programs from getting any processing time. Returns the previous mode. **Example:**

    prevmode = Exclusive(@ON)

Execute (statement)   Allows you to execute a batch statement in a protected environment. If an error occurs, you can recover from it. This is ideal for letting users execute a statement without risking an abort of the batch file. **Example:**

    usercmd = ""
    usercmd = AskLine("Batch Executer", "What batch file would you like to execute?",usercmd)
    Execute Call(usercmd,"")

Exit   Causes the batch file to stop executing. Used to quit a batch file without processing it all the way to the end.

FileAppend(sourcelist, destination)   Copies one or more source files onto the end of the destination file. **Example:**

    FileAppend("*.bat", "batch.lst")

FileClose(filehandle)   Closes a file that has been opened. Takes as an argument the filehandle returned from FileOpen. **Example:**

    handle = FileOpen("junk.txt","READ")
    FileClose(handle)

FileCopy(sourcelist, destination, @TRUE ¦ @FALSE)
Copies a file or files. May display a warning message before overwriting an existing file if desired. Uses multiple source files separated with a space. Wildcards may also be used. **Example:**

    FileCopy("c:\junk.tmp c:\temp\junk.txt",
    "c:\garbage\junk.*", @FALSE)

FileDelete(filelist)   Deletes the specified files if they are not read-only. Will return an error if the file is a hidden or system file, or if the file does not exist. Returns @TRUE if successful, @FALSE if not.

Wildcards are acceptable, and you can separate filenames with spaces. **Example:**

```
FileDelete("*.bak *.bk? *.tmp")
```

FileExist((d:)(path)filename)   Tests to see if a file exists. Returns @TRUE if it does exist, @FALSE if not. Use this to make your batch files more bulletproof, since many Windows Batch Language commands will cause a fatal error if the file doesn't exist. **Example:**

```
delfile = FileExist("swap.sw2")
If delfile == @TRUE Then FileDelete("swap.sw2")
```

FileExtension(filename)   Takes as its argument a string whose value is a filename and, optionally its path, including its extension, and returns a string whose value is the extension. **Example:**

```
filevar = AskLine("FileView", "What file did you want to view?", "")
filext = FileExtension(filevar)
If (filext == "exe") || (filext == "com") Then Goto Sorry
Run("nviewer.exe", filevar)
Exit
:Sorry
Message("Sorry", "Sorry, but there isn't really anything to see with an executable file.")
```

FileItemize(filelist)   Takes a list of filenames, wildcards allowed, and returns a complete list of files that meets the criteria, separated by spaces. Especially useful with *ItemSelect*, which takes a list of items separated by spaces as its argument. **Example:**

```
;Choose from a list of files to edit when starting
;Word Perfect.
wpfiles = FileItemize("c:\wp51\ndw\*.chp")
editfile = ItemSelect("Which Chapter?", wpfiles, " ")
Run("wp.pif",editfile)
```

FileLocate(filename)   Searches for a file in the current directory, or anywhere along the DOS path. Returns the full filename, including complete path. **Example:**

```
editfile = FileLocate("ndw.ini")
Run("notepad.exe", editfile)
```

FileMove(sourcelist, destination, @TRUE ¦ @FALSE)
Copies a file or files, and deletes the source file(s). May display a warning message before overwriting an existing file, if desired. To move multiple source files, separate them with a space. You may use wildcards. Use @TRUE if a warning is to be issued before overwriting an existing file, and @FALSE if no warning is desired. Returns @TRUE if successful, @FALSE if not. **Example:**

```
FileMove("c:\win\*.ini", "d:\winfiles", @TRUE)
```

FileOpen(filename, "READ" ¦ "WRITE")   Used to open a file for use by the FileRead or FileWrite functions. The file must be an ASCII file. The function returns a special integer value (filehandle) which can then be used by the FileRead, FileWrite, or FileClose functions. When finished reading from or writing to the file, use FileClose to close it. **Example:**

```
; Opens autoexec.bat for reading, with a filehandle
; assigned to the variable "filevar".
filevar = FileOpen("c:\autoexec.bat", "READ")
```

FilePath(filename)   Takes a full filename, including path, and strips out the filename, leaving only the path portion. **Example:**

```
ini = FileLocate("win.ini")
inipath = FilePath(ini)
```

FileRead(filehandle)   Returns a line of text as a single string each time it is invoked. When the end of the file is reached, it returns "*EOF*". The file to read from is identified by the filehandle returned by the FileOpen function. **Example:**

```
filevar = FileOpen ("junk.txt", "READ")
:begin
```

LineOfText = FileRead(filevar) Display (3, "Junk.Txt", LineOfText)

If LineOfText != "*EOF*" Then Goto begin

FileClose (filevar)

FileRename(sourcelist, destination)   Changes the name of a file or files. You can use wildcards in the source list, and the * wildcard for the destination. Unlike FileMove, you cannot rename across drives. **Example:**

FileRename ("c:\autoexec.bat", "autoexec.sav")

FileRoot(filename)   Takes a filename, including its extension, and strips out the period and the extension, returning only the root, including the full pathname if it was part of the filename. **Example:**

inifile = FileLocate("win.ini")

iniroot = FileRoot(inifile)

FileSize(filelist)   Takes a list of files, separated by spaces, as its argument, and returns the total of the bytes taken by the files. Does not accept wildcards, but you can use FileItemize to generate the list. **Example:**

baksize = FileSize(FileItemize ("*.bak"))

Display(4,"Space Wasted by BAK files", baksize)

FileWrite(filehandle,outputtext)   Writes a line of text to an ASCII file each time it is invoked. The file to write to is identified by the filehandle returned from the FileOpen function. **Example:**

stuff = AskLine("Stuff to Write", "What would you like to write in STUFF.TXT? ", "")

filevar = FileOpen("stuff.txt", "WRITE")

FileWrite (filevar,stuffadd) FileClose(filevar)

Goto *label*   Causes the batch file to branch, unconditionally, to the line identified by the label. Labels begin with a colon in the first position of the line, and must not include any embedded spaces. **Example:**

If WinExist("WordPerfect") == @FALSE Then Goto openwp

```
WinActivate("WordPerfect")
Goto end
:openwp
Run("wp.pif", "")
:end
```

If *condition* Then *statement* Used to test for the value of a condition, and if that condition is true, then a statement will be executed. If the condition is false, then the statement is skipped, and the next line of the batch file is executed. **Example:**

```
If WinExist("Notepad") == @TRUE Then Goto activate
inifile = FileItemize("c:\win\*.ini")
editfile = ItemSelect("Which .INI File?", inifile, " ")
Run("notepad.exe",editfile)
Goto end
:activate
WinActivate("Notepad")
:end
```

IgnoreInput(@TRUE ¦ @FALSE) Causes Windows to ignore all mouse movements and keystrokes when set to @TRUE. Returns to normal by setting to @FALSE. Use with extreme caution, because a mistake will crash the computer! **Example:**

```
IgnoreInput(@TRUE)
Display(15,"PATIENCE!", "This will take 15 seconds, and
nothing you can do will make it faster!")
IgnoreInput(@FALSE)
```

● **NOTE** This does not work in version 1.00.

IniRead(section, keyname, default) Allows you to read data from the WIN.INI file. If the specified data is not found, returns the default string. **Example:**

```
beepstat = IniRead("windows", "Beep", "Yes")
If beepstat == "No" Then Goto beepoff
```

```
Beep
Beep
Beep
Goto end
:beepoff
Display(3,"BEEP!", "You have Beeps turned OFF!")
:end
```

IniReadPvt(section, keyname, default, filename)   Allows you to read data from a private .INI file. Works like IniRead. **Example:**

```
save = IniReadPvt("CONFIGURATION", "SAVE", "TRUE",
"ndw.ini")
```

IniWrite(section, keyname, data)   Allows you to write data to your WIN.INI file. If the section is not found, it will create it. If the keyname is already present, it will overwrite it. **Example:**

```
IniWrite("windows", "Beep", "yes")
```

IniWritePvt(section, keyname, data, filename)   Allows you to write data to a private .INI file. Works like IniWrite. **Example:**

```
IniWritePvt("boot", "shell", "c:\ndw\ndw.exe",
"c:\win\system.ini")
```

IsDefined(var)   Tests to see if a variable is currently defined. If it is, it returns @TRUE. If it has never been defined, or has been dropped, it returns @FALSE. **Example:**

```
defined = IsDefined(anyvar)
If defined == @TRUE Then Goto OK
anyvar = AskLine("Definition", "What is the value of
ANYVAR?", "something")
:OK
```

IsKeyDown(keycode)   Used to test the current state of the Shift or Ctrl key. If the specified key is held down, @YES is returned.

If the key is not, @NO is returned. Accepts the right mouse button for Shift, and the left button for Ctrl. **Example:**

> ;The following requires both the Shift and the Ctrl keys
> ;to be pressed.
> IsKeyDown(@CTRL & @SHIFT) ;
> This one only requires that the Ctrl key be pressed
> IsKeyDown(@CTRL)
> ;And this one accepts either key
> IsKeyDown(@CTRL | @SHIFT)

IsNumber(stringvar)   Checks a string, and tests whether it is valid as an integer. Used for checking user input before acting on it. Returns @YES if it is an integer, @NO if it is not. **Example:**

> :getnum
> int = AskLine("How Many", "How many times should I do this?", "1")
> If IsNumber(int) == @NO Then Goto getnum

ItemCount(list, delimiter)   Counts the number of items in a list. Takes the list and a delimiter as its arguments. **Example:**

> dirlist = DirItemize("c:*")
> dircount = ItemCount(dirlist, " ")
> Display(3, "INFO", "There are %dircount% directories.")

ItemExtract(position, list, delimiter)   Evaluates a list and extracts an item from it, based on its position in the list. **Example:**

> filelist = FileItemize("*.*")
> first = ItemExtract(1, filelist, " ")

ItemSelect(title, list, delimiter)   Draws a list box, and allows user to select an item from the list. Returns a string whose value is the item selected from the list. **Example:**

> inifile = FileItemize("c:\win*.ini")
> editfile = ItemSelect("Which .INI File?", inifile, " ")
> Run("notepad.exe",editfile)

LastError( )   Returns the error code for the most recent error. Will not work with fatal errors, because they will cancel execution of the batch file. **Example:**

    ErrorMode(@OFF)
    close = WinClose("Notepad")
    If close == @True Then Goto end
    If LastError( ) == 1039 Then Display(2,"ERROR",
    "Window wasn't open!")
    :end

LogDisk(drive)   Changes disk drives. Returns @TRUE if successful, @FALSE if not. **Example:**

    LogDisk("e:")

Max(integer(, integer) …)   Evaluates a list of integers, separated by commas, and returns the largest integer in the list. **Example:**

    maxnum = Max(17, –23, 45, 6)
    Display(3, "Largest number is:", maxnum)

Message(title, text)   Displays a message until the user clicks on **OK**. Unlike Display, it stops processing indefinitely. **Example:**

    Message("The current path is:", Environment ("PATH"))

Min(integer(, integer) …)   Evaluates a list of integers, separated by commas, and returns the smallest. **Example:**

    minnum = Min(17, –23, 45, 6)
    Display(3, "Smallest number is:", minnum)

Num2Char(integer)   Used to change an integer to its ASCII equivalent. Accepts any integer from 0 to 255. Extremely useful for converting control codes to a string for inclusion in string variables. **Example:**

    crlf = StrCat(Num2Char(13), Num2Char(10))
    Message("Two Line Box", "This is a line of text. %crlf%This
    is another line of text.")

ParseData(string)   Chops a string up into substrings. Assumes
spaces are the delimiter, and stores each "word" in param1, param2
… param*n*, with the total count (*n*) stored in param0. **Example:**

```
crlf = StrCat(Num2Char(13), Num2Char(10))
user = AskLine("NAME?", "What is your name, please?",
"Jane Doe")
ParseData(user)
If param0 == 1 Then Goto single
If param0 == 2 Then Goto double
name = param3
Goto end
:single
name = param1
Goto end
:double
name = param2
:end
Message("UserName", " Since we are rather formal
here, %crlf% your name on this system will be:
%name%")
```

Pause(title, text)   Draws a message box, and Displays a text
message in it until the user selects either OK, or Cancel. This is
similar to the Message instruction, except for the Cancel option, and
the inclusion of an exclamation-point icon. **Example:**

```
Pause("Ready?", "Insert disk to copy into Drive A:")
```

Random(max)   Takes a maximum number as its parameter,
and returns a pseudorandom positive number less than that maximum. **Example:**

```
ran = Random(126)
Display(3,"Random number less than 126", ran)
```

Return   Returns control to the calling batch file. If there is no calling batch file, then Exit is performed.

Run(programname, parameters)   Starts a program in its normal window. If the program is not an executable file (.COM, .EXE, .BAT, .PIF) then it must have an association to an executable file. If the file has an extension of .EXE, then the extension may be omitted. **Example:**

> Run("notepad", "win.ini")
> Run("c:\ndw\editfile.wbt", "*.ini")

RunHide(programname, parameters)   Same as Run, except that it attempts to run the program in a hidden window. **Example:**

> RunHide("sleeper", "")

RunIcon(programname, parameters)   Same as Run, except that it iconizes the program. **Example:**

> ;Run AfterDark as an icon
> RunIcon("ad","")

RunZoom(programname, parameters)   Same as Run, except that it zooms the program to full screen. **Example:**

> RunZoom("c:\borland\vision.exe","")

SendKey(charstring)   Used to pass keystrokes to the active program. Can be used to send any alphanumeric character, as well as the punctuation marks and special characters shown in Table B.1. **Example:**

> ;Open Borland's Object Vision, and go to the
> ;File Open menu, looking for *.OVD files
> RunIcon("c:\borland\vision.exe", "")
> SendKey("!FO*.ovd")

SKDebug(mode)   Controls the debug mode of SendKey. If SKDebug is set to @ON, the keystrokes are sent to both the application and a file. If set to @PARSEONLY, it sends the keystrokes to the file, but not to the application. If set to the default, @OFF, then it sends the keystrokes only to the application. The default filename for

Table B.1: Special Characters for SendKey

Key	Send Key Equivalent
~	{~}
!	{!}
^	{^}
+	{+}
Backspace	{BACKSPACE} or {BS}
Break	{BREAK}
Clear	{CLEAR}
Delete	{DELETE} or {DEL}
Down Arrow	{DOWN}
End {END} Enter	{ENTER} or ~
Escape	{ESCAPE} or {ESC}
F1 through F16	{F1} through {F16}
Help	{HELP}
Home	{HOME}
Insert	{INSERT}
Left Arrow	{LEFT}
Page Down	{PGDN}
Page Up	{PGUP}
Print Screen	{PRTSC]
Right Arrow	{RIGHT}
Space	{SPACE} or {SP}
Tab {TAB}	
Up Arrow	{UP}

To enter an Alt, Shift, or Ctrl key combination use the following symbols before the character you want. Alt = ! (exclamation point); Shift = + (plus sign); Control = ^ (caret).

SKDebug to use is C:\@@SKDBUG.TXT, but this can be controlled by making an entry in WIN.INI, such as:

```
(Batch Runner)
SKDFile=c:\win\debug.key
```

Example:

```
Run("wp.pif", "")
If WinConfig( ) & 32 Then Goto enhanced
Goto end
:enhanced
SKDebug (@ON)
;You can only pass keystrokes in 386 Enhanced
;mode to a DOS Application.
SendKey ("{F5}")
SKDebug (@OFF)
:end
```

StrCat(string1, string2(, string3) ...) Joins two or more strings together into a single string. **Example:**

```
crlf = StrCat(Num2Char(13), Num2Char(10))
```

StrCmp(string1, string2) Evaluates and compares two strings. Requires an exact match, including case. Returns −1 if string1 is less than string2, 0 if they are the same, and 1 if string1 is greater than string2, using ANSI equivalency for the test. Note that the same thing can be accomplished using the relational operators, >, ≥, ==, !=, <, ≤. Example:

```
filename = AskLine("Edit Filename", "What File would
you like to Edit?", "WIN.INI")
If StrCmp(StrLower(filename), "win.ini") != 0 Then Goto
notini
Run("notepad",filename)
```

```
Goto end
:notini
editor = AskLine("Editor?", "What editor would you like
to use?", "")
Run(editor, filename)
:end
```

StrFill(fillstr, length)   Builds a filler string of specified length using substring as the filler. **Example:**

```
Display(3,"Money!", StrFill("$", 60))
```

StrFix(initstring, padstring, length)   Creates a string of the specified length either by padding the initial string with the padding string, or by chopping off the initial string at the specified length, counting from the left. **Example:**

```
name = StrFix("Frank", "*", 20) Display(5,"",name)
```

StrICmp(string1, string2)   Like StrCmp, but it is not case-sensitive. Returns −1 if string1 is less than string2, 0 if they are the same, and 1 if string1 is greater than string2, using ANSI equivalency for the test. **Example:**

```
If StrICmp("Alfie", "ALFIE") == 0 Then Goto SAME
Message("Compare", "Alfie is not the same as ALFIE.")
Exit
:SAME
Message("Compare", "Alfie is the same as ALFIE.")
```

StrIndex(string, substring, start, direction)   Searches for a substring of a string, and returns the position the substring was found. Returns 0 if the string is not found. Can search in either direction, starting from any point in the string. To start at the beginning, direction will be @FWDSCAN and start position will be 0. To start at the end of the string, direction will be @BACKSCAN and start position will be 0. **Example:**

```
strvar = AskLine("String Index", "Type a sentence:", "")
start = 1
end = StrIndex(strvar, " ", start, @FWDSCAN)
```

```
word = StrSub(strvar, start, end − 1)
Message("String Index", "The first word is: %word%.")
```

StrLen(string)   Evaluates a string and returns an integer whose value is the length of the string. **Example:**

```
strvar = AskLine("String Length", "Type in a sentence or two.", "")
length = StrLen(strvar)
Message("String Length", "The string you typed in is %length% characters long.")
```

StrLower(string)   Changes a string to all lower case. **Example:**

```
StrLower("This is a SilLY sTRinG Which NEEds tO be fIXeD.")
```

StrReplace(string, old, new)   Does a search and replace. Changes all occurrences of one string with another. **Example:**

```
filelist = FileItemize("*.wbt")
crlf = StrCat(Num2Char(13), Num2Char(10))
newlist = StrReplace (filelist, " ", crlf)
filevar = FileOpen("wbatlist.txt", "WRITE")
FileWrite(filevar, newlist)
FileClose(filevar)
TextBox("Windows Batch Files", "wbatlist.txt")
```

StrScan(string, delimiters, start, direction)   Evaluates a string, looking for a particular delimiter or set of delimiters. Returns the position of the first occurrence found; if not found, returns 0. **Example:**

```
strvar = AskLine("String Scan", "Enter a series of numbers, separated by commas or semicolons.", "")
firstnum = StrScan(strvar, ",;", 1, @FWDSCAN)
Display(3, "String Scan", "The first number is %firstnum%.")
```

StrSub(string, start, length)   Evaluates a string, and extracts a substring from within it. **Example:**

```
strvar = AskLine("SubString", "Enter a sentence,
please.", "")
firstword = StrSub(strvar, 1, StrScan(strvar, " ", 1,
@FWDSCAN))
Display(3, "First Word", "The first word is: %firstword%")
```

StrTrim(string)   Strips all leading and trailing spaces from a string. Use it to clean up user input where it could be a problem, such as with a filename. **Example:**

```
filename = StrTrim(StrLower(AskLine("File?", "Enter the file
to edit?", "")))
```

StrUpper(string)   Evaluates a string, and changes it all to upper case. **Example:**

```
response = StrUpper(AskLine("Proceed?", "Type yes to
proceed, all else cancels", "NO"))
If response != "YES" Then Exit
```

TextBox(title, filename)   Draws a list box, and displays a file in it. It also allows the user to select a line, which it then returns to the batch file. TextBox will search the DOS path if the file specified is not found in the current drive and directory. **Example:**

```
var = TextBox ("Choose a Line", "c:\autoexec.bat")
Display(3,"Chosen Line", var)
```

Version( )   Finds the current version of BATCHRUN.EXE. **Example:**

```
batver = Version()
Display(3,"Current Version", "The current version of
BatchRunner is: %batver%")
```

WallPaper(bmpname, tile)   Changes the current wallpaper used on the desktop, and determines if it is to be tiled or not. **Example:**

```
filelist = FileItemize("c:\win\*.bmp")
bmpvar = ItemSelect("Select your new background",
filelist, " ")
```

WallPaper(bmpvar, @FALSE)

WinActivate(partialwindowname)   Activates the specified window or icon, making it the current window. The most recently used window or icon that matches the partial window name used is activated. If the specified window is an icon it restores it; if it is already a window, it makes it the current window, but does not change the size. Note that this function requires an exact match of the partial window name, and is case-sensitive. Returns @TRUE if successful, @FALSE if not. **Example:**

```
If WinExist("WordPerfect") Then Goto activate
Run("wp.pif", "")
Goto end
:activate
WinActivate("WordPerfect")
:end
```

WinArrange(style)   Arranges all open windows on the desktop, up to 12 open windows. Does not rearrange iconized windows. Accepts one of five different styles, @STACK, @TILE, @AR-RANGE (same as @TILE), @ROWS, and @COLUMNS. **Example:**

WinArrange(@TILE)

WinClose(partialwindowname)   Closes a window or icon. Like WinActivate, it takes a partial window name, which must be an exact match, and which is case-sensitive. Returns @TRUE if successful, @FALSE if not. **Example:**

WinClose("Notepad")

WinConfig( )   Returns the sum of Windows mode flags. These flags are the following:

1	Protected mode
2	80286 CPU
4	80386 CPU
8	80486 CPU
16	Standard mode

32	Enhanced mode
64	8086 CPU
128	80186 CPU
256	Large PageFrame
512	Small PageFrame
1024	Math Coprocessor installed

Example

```
currentcfg = WinConfig()
If currentcfg & 8 Then Display(3,"CPU", "This machine
has an 80486 Processor.")
```

WinExist(partialwindowname)   Checks for the presence of a particular window or icon. Returns @TRUE if found, @FALSE if not. Example:

```
If WinExist("QPro") == @FALSE Then Run("QP.PIF", "")
```

WinGetActive( )   Finds the title of the currently active window. Example:

```
curwin = WinGetActive
```

WinHide(partialwindowname)   Used to hide a window or icon. When hidden, the programs continue to run. A partial window name of " " causes the current window to be hidden. Returns @TRUE if successful, @FALSE if not. **Example:**

```
WinHide("Sleeper")
```

WinIconize(partialwindowname)   Minimizes a window. Like WinHide, a partial window name of " " causes the currently active window to be iconized. Returns @TRUE if successful, @FALSE if not. Example:

```
Run("clock.exe", "")
WinIconize("Clo")
```

WinItemize( )   Creates a list of the titles of all open windows, separated by tabs. Behaves similarly to FileItemize and DirItemize, except for the use of tabs as delimiters, because window titles can have embedded spaces. **Example:**

```
winopen = WinItemize()
winchoose = ItemSelect ("Windows", winopen,
Num2Char(9))
WinActive(winchoose)
```

WinPlace(x-ulc, y-ulc, x-brc, y-brc, partialwin-downame)

Places the window in a specified location, and sets the size as well. Size is controlled by 4 parameters: x-ulc, the distance from the upper left corner of the window to the left of the screen (0–1000); y-ulc, the distance from the upper left corner of the window to the top of the screen (0–1000); x-brc, the distance from the bottom right corner of the window to the left of the screen (10–1000, or @NORESIZE); and y-brc, the distance from the bottom right corner of the window to the top of the screen (10–1000, or @NORESIZE or @ABOVEICONS). **Example:**

```
WinPlace(700,0,200,200,"Clock")
```

WinPosition(partialwindowname)

Finds the coordinates of the specified window. **Example:**

```
WinPosition("Clock")
```

WinShow(partialwindowname)

Returns the specified window to normal size and position. **Example:**

```
WinShow("PageMaker")
```

WinTitle(partialwindowname, newname)

Renames window or icon by changing its window title. Returns @TRUE if successful, @FALSE if not. **Caution:** Some programs will not behave well if their window title is changed, so use caution with this function. **Example:**

```
WinTitle("QPro", "Quattro Pro 3.0")
```

WinVersion(@MAJOR | @MINOR)

Finds what version of Windows is running. @MAJOR returns the integer portion of the version, and @MINOR returns the decimal portion. **Example:**

```
ver = WinVersion(@MINOR)
```

Message("Version", StrCat("Windows Version 3.", ver))

WinWaitClose(partialwindowname)   Halts the running of the batch file while it waits for the specified window or icon to close. Closes all windows or icons which match the partial window name. Returns @TRUE if successful, @FALSE if not.

WinZoom(partialwindowname)   Zooms a window to full screen. Returns @TRUE if successful, @FALSE if not. **Example:**

WinZoom("Note")

Yield   Provides clock cycles for other windows to do processing. This is one way to make your batch files better behaved, allowing other Windows processes to also run.

Appendix C

The Emergency Diskette Programs

The Emergency Diskette programs are to be run from the DOS prompt. If you are trying to repair or restore your hard disk or to recover deleted files, the programs must be run from a floppy drive because:

- Norton Disk Doctor and Speed Disk cannot be run safely in a multi-tasking environment such as Windows.

- If you have deleted unprotected files, starting Windows to run UnErase can cause the files to be overwritten and, therefore, make them unrecoverable.

- If you have accidentally formatted your hard disk, you will not be able to access UnFormat if it is (or was) on your hard disk. It can be run only from a floppy.

NORTON DISK DOCTOR

Disk Doctor should be used in the following cases:

- when you have trouble accessing a disk or a disk behaves erratically;

- when files or directories seem to be missing but were not deleted;

- when you want to practice preventive maintenance to look for budding problems.

To Diagnose a Disk

1. Insert the Emergency Diskette into the floppy drive. Change to that drive. At the DOS prompt, key in

ndd

2. In the Norton Disk Doctor window, click on **Diagnose Disk.**

3. Click on the **drive(s)** that you want to test. Use the space bar to select and deselect drives. A checkmark will appear beside the selected drives.

4. Click on **Diagnose** or press **Enter**. The tests being performed will be listed on the screen with checkmarks appearing next to the tests as they are completed. The following parts of the hard disk are tested:

Partition Table   Information on how the hard disk is divided.

Boot Record   The portion of the disk that identifies the disk and contains the programs from which DOS boots.

FAT   The File Allocation Table where file locations are tracked.

Directory Structure   Information about directory organization.

File Structure   Information about the organization of the files.

Lost Clusters   Clusters that are recorded in the FAT but do not belong to a file or directory.

5.   If errors are detected and you want Disk Doctor to correct them, create an UnDo file just in case the changes that take place are not quite what you expect.

6.   When the Surface Test window opens, select the **tests** you wish to perform. To change the Surface Test default options, see *To Set Disk Doctor Options,* below.

7.   When the tests are finished, select **Report**... from the Summary window to generate a report of the test results. Save and/or print the report to keep a record of the tests that have been performed.

To UnDo Changes

1.   Start Disk Doctor. Select **UnDo Changes** from the Norton Disk Doctor window.

2.   Read the explanation and if you want to continue, select **Yes.**

3.   Select the **drive** where the undo information was previously stored and click on **OK.** Follow the instructions to undo the Disk Doctor operations.

To Set Disk Doctor Options

1.   Start Disk Doctor. Select **Options** in the Norton Disk Doctor window.

2.   In the Disk Doctor Options window, select the **options** that you want to configure.

3.   When finished, select **Save Settings** to make your choices permanent.

● OPTIONS–SURFACE TESTS

Choose **Surface Test** to change the default settings.

Test   Select **Disk Test** to test the entire disk. Select **File Test** to test only the areas being used by existing files. Note that Disk Test is slower, but more thorough than File Test.

Test Type   The Daily option is a quick scan. The Weekly option is slower but more thorough. The Auto Weekly is the default setting and is a daily test except on Fridays, when the Weekly test is performed.

Passes   Select **Repetitions** and key in the **number of passes** to specify the number of times Disk Doctor will search the disk. For an extended test, select **Continuous** and the search will proceed until you press **Esc** to end it.

Repair Setting   Select **Don't Repair** if you want a diagnosis but do not want any fixes. Select **Prompt before Repairing** and Disk Doctor will report the error and ask if you want the error fixed. If you want Disk Doctor to make repairs without prompting, choose **Repair Automatically**.

● OPTIONS–CUSTOM MESSAGE

When Disk Doctor finds an error, it displays an error and correction message. To substitute your own message, select **Custom Message.** Note that after a custom message is displayed, the user cannot proceed and will be returned to the Main menu after selecting **OK.**

● OPTIONS–TESTS TO SKIP

This allows you to specify which Disk Doctor tests you would like to skip. Use the mouse or space bar to toggle the check boxes on and off.

Skip Partition Tests   Toggle this option on if your system uses nonstandard partition software.

Skip CMOS Tests   Select this option if you are using a non-standard CMOS format.

Skip Surface Tests   Toggle this option on if you always want to skip surface testing.

Only 1 Hard Disk   Check this option if your computer reports more than one hard disk and you have only one.

● **NOTE**   You can run the Disk Doctor from a network but you will not be able to test network drives. Also, Norton Disk Doctor will not work on disks having 1,024 or more cylinders.

To Use Disk Doctor from the Command Line

SYNTAX

NDD [drive:]… [/C] [/Q] [/R[A]:pathname] [/X:drives]

NDD [drive:]… [/REBUILD]

NDD [drive]… [/UNDELETE]

> **drive**   Specifies the disk drive to be diagnosed or repaired. More than one drive can be listed.

> **/C**   Specifies a complete test including the partition table, boot record, root directory, lost clusters, and the default surface tests.

> **/Q**   Specifies all tests except the surface tests.

> **/R[A]:pathname**   Writes (or appends) a report of the tests performed to the named file.

> **/X:drives**   Excludes named drives from testing.

> **/REBUILD**   Rebuilds a destroyed disk.

> **/UNDELETE**   Undeletes a previously skipped DOS partition.

SPEED DISK

Speed Disk is a disk optimization program that rearranges files and directories to minimize the movement of the hard disk read-write heads. Make sure to back up your files as a safety measure before running Speed Disk on your computer for the first time.

To Run Speed Disk

1. Insert the Eemergency Diskette into the appropriate floppy drive. Change to that drive. At the DOS prompt, key in

   speedisk

2. The program will ask you to select a drive to optimize. Select a **drive** and click on **OK.**

3. After searching the drive, Speed Disk will ask if you want to optimize the drive or to configure Speed Disk.

4. If you select Optimize, the program will continue and inform you of its findings. If you want to change the Speed Disk settings, select Configure.

● OPTIONS–CONFIGURE MENU

Directory Order… Lets you select the order of directories on the disk.

File Sort… Allows you to select the sort criteria for files within directories. The default is unsorted.

Files To Place First… Opens a dialog box in which you can specify files to be placed at the front of the disk.

Unmovable Files… Specifies files, such as some copy-protected files, that should not be moved by Speed Disk.

Other Options… **Read After Write:** If on, data will be read back at once after it is written to verify accuracy. The default is on. Speed Disk will work faster if it is toggled off. **Clear un-used space:** Writes zeroes in all unused clusters after optimization as a security measure. **Beep when done:** Sounds a beep when optimization is complete.

Save Options to Disk Saves the current set of Speed Disk options to SD.INI, a hidden file in the root directory of the currently selected disk. These options will be in effect when you select a different disk and each time that you start up Speed Disk. The options saved are these: the optimization method; the physical directory and file placement; the file sort criterion; selection of immovable files; the verification method; and the clear unused space option.

• OPTIONS–INFORMATION MENU

Disk Statistics... Provides a report on the chosen drive, including the size of the drive, space used, clusters allocated, and so forth.

Map Legend... Provides a detailed disk map legend.

Show Static Files... Reports on files that Speed Disk has determined as unmovable during disk optimization.

Walk Map... Select this option to see which files occupy which clusters on the disk map. Use the mouse or cursor control keys to "walk" around the map. Press **Esc** to return to the menu.

Fragmentation Report... Provides a report on which files are fragmented and to what degree.

• OPTIONS–OPTIMIZE MENU

Begin Optimization Starts the optimization process.

Drive... Select to change the drive choice.

Optimization Method... Allows you to select from the following five methods to optimize your disk:

- **Full Optimization** defragments all files without rearranging the directory or file sort. This method will fill all empty spaces between files.

- **Full with DIRs first** defragments files and moves directories to the front.

- **Full with File reorder** performs a full optimization of the disk, reordering files by directory. This is the most thorough and also the slowest method of optimization.

- **Unfragment Files Only** will unfragment as many files as possible. Not all holes will be filled and some large files may not be unfragmented.

- **Unfragment Free Space** will fill in free space but will not unfragment files.

To Use Speed Disk from the Command Line

SYNTAX

SPEEDISK [drive:] [/F ¦ /FD ¦ /FF] [/Sorder] [/V] [/B]

SPEEDISK [drive:] [/Q ¦ /U] [/V] [/B]

/F	Full optimization
/FD	Full optimization, directories in front
/FF	Full optimization, files reordered
/Q	Unfragment free space (fastest option)
/U	Unfragment files only
/S	Sort files in the order specified
Order	One of the following:

N   Name

E   Extension

D   Date and time

S   Size

Add a minus sign (–) to make the sort in reverse order

/B	Reboot after optimization is complete
/V	After writing, verify by reading back immediately

UNERASE

UnErase can recover files automatically if they have remained intact. Files also can be recovered manually if they have become fragmented or have been partially overwritten.

To Automatically Recover Erased Files

1. Insert the Emergency Diskette in the floppy drive. Change to that drive. From the DOS prompt, key in

   unerase

2. In the UnErase window, pull down the File menu to select the drive and directory you want.

3. Highlight the file to be recovered and click on the **UnErase button.**

4. Enter the first letter of the filename. The file will be automatically recovered.

• OPTIONS–FILE MENU

View Current Directory   Shows erased files in the current directory, including subdirectories.

View All Directories   Shows all erased files in all directories on the current drive.

Change Drive...   Opens a dialog box to allow you to change drives.

Change Directory...   Opens a dialog box containing the directory tree.

Select   Tags the currently highlighted file. Tagged files are recovered when you select the UnErase button.

Select Group...   Allows you to key in a file specification. DOS wildcards "*' and "?" can be used. Press **Enter** to tag all the files matching the specification.

Unselect Group...   Key in a **file specification** including DOS wildcards "*" and "?". Press **Enter** and all the files matching the specification that are tagged, will be untagged.

Rename   Key in a new name for the unerased file or directory.

UnErase To...   Specifies a new drive destination for the unerased file.

Append To...   Adds the contents of the selected file to the specified file.

Manual UnErase... See *To UnErase Files Manually*.

Create File Creates a new file. Use when the file is intact but its directory is missing.

● OPTIONS–SEARCH MENU

For Data Types Searches the erased files looking for particular data types such as Lotus 1-2-3 files, dBase files, and others. Use the space bar to toggle on your selections.

For Text Enter a string of text. UnErase will search the erased files for any files that contain the string. The search is not case-sensitive.

For Lost Names See *To UnErase a File from an Erased Directory*.

Set Search Range Allows you to set a starting and ending cluster number to limit the search.

Continue Search Resumes a search that has been interrupted.

● OPTIONS MENU

Select the way in which you would like the erased files to be sorted. You can sort by name, extension, time, size, directory, and prognosis. The prognosis is an indication of how likely recovery is for a particular file. The prognosis can be Excellent, Good, Average, Poor, Not Applicable, or Recovered.

You can also toggle on the option: Include nonerased files. With this option on, the display will include all files on the selected drive, whether erased or not.

To UnErase a File from an Erased Directory

1. Start UnErase.

2. Select **Lost Names** from the Search menu.

3. Highlight the file you want and click on the UnErase button. Provide a first letter for the filename. The file will be recovered automatically.

To UnErase Files Manually

1. Start UnErase. From the File menu change to the directory where the erased files are located. Click on **View** for the list of erased files in the highlighted directory.

2. Highlight the file you want to recover and select **Manual UnErase** from the File menu.

3. Key in a **first character** for the erased filename. Select **Add Cluster.**

4. Select one of the four options to add clusters to the file.

5. Click on **View File** to view the contents of the file as you go though them. Or select **View Map** to see the area on the disk occupied by the assembled clusters. Select **OK** when finished viewing.

6. Select **Save** to save the recovered file.

● OPTIONS–MANUAL UNERASE

All clusters   UnErase will add all clusters likely to be part of the file.

Next probable   Will add only the next cluster that is probably part of the file.

Data search   To search for a specific string of text.

Cluster number   To add a cluster when the cluster number is known.

If you choose Data Search, in the Data Search dialog box, key in the text and select the **Find button.** Toggle off the Ignore case button if you want the search to be case-sensitive. Select **Add Cluster** if you want to add the cluster containing the match to the existing file.

If you select Cluster Number, at the Starting Cluster prompt, key in the first number of the range of clusters you want to add. At the Ending Cluster prompt, key in the last number of the range. Select **OK.**

To Use UnErase from the Command Line

SYNTAX

UNERASE [pathname] [/IMAGE] [/MIRROR] [/NOTRACK]

/IMAGE   Use the Image recovery information (excludes MIRROR).

/MIRROR   Use the MIRROR recovery information (excludes IMAGE).

/NOTRACK   Exclude Delete Tracking information.

UNFORMAT

UnFormat can recover data from a hard disk that has been formatted or damaged by a virus or power failure. UnFormat also can recover a diskette that has been formatted with Safe Format.

To Unformat a Hard Disk

1. Insert a bootable diskette with the same DOS version used to format your disk in drive A:. Reboot your system.

2. Remove the DOS diskette, insert the Emergency Disk in drive A: and key in

    a:unformat

3. Read the message in the UnFormat dialog box and click on **Continue.**

4. Select the drive you wish to unformat and click on **OK.**

5. You will be asked if IMAGE or MIRROR was previously used to save information on the drive to be unformatted. Select **Yes** or **No,** as appropriate.

6. Select **Yes** in the confirmation box.

7. If you answered Yes in step 5, and the information has been saved, the IMAGE or MIRROR information will display. Click on **OK.** Select **Yes** in the Absolutely Sure box. Then select **Full** in the Full or Partial Restore box.

If you answered Yes in step 5 and the IMAGE or MIRROR information is not available, select **Yes** to proceed with the unformat without IMAGE or MIRROR information.

If you answered No in step 5, go to step 8.

8.   Click on OK, once or twice, until the unformat is complete.

● **NOTE**   You can select a partial restoration in step 7. Toggle on Boot Record, File Allocation Table, or Root Directory to select these areas to be restored.

Index

G

Selections from The SYBEX Library

UTILITIES

The Computer Virus Protection Handbook
Colin Haynes
192pp. Ref. 696-0
This book is the equivalent of an intensive emergency preparedness seminar on computer viruses. Readers learn what viruses are, how they are created, and how they infect systems. Step-by-step procedures help computer users to identify vulnerabilities, and to assess the consequences of a virus infection. Strategies on coping with viruses, as well as methods of data recovery, make this book well worth the investment.

Mastering the Norton Utilities 5
Peter Dyson
400pp, Ref. 725-8
This complete guide to installing and using the Norton Utilities 5 is a must for beginning and experienced users alike. It offers a clear, detailed description of each utility, with options, uses and examples—so users can quickly identify the programs they need and put Norton right to work. Includes valuable coverage of the newest Norton enhancements.

Mastering PC Tools Deluxe 6
For Versions 5.5 and 6.0
425pp, Ref. 700-2
An up-to-date guide to the lifesaving utilities in PC Tools Deluxe version 6.0 from installation, to high-speed back-ups, data recovery, file encryption, desktop applications, and more. Includes detailed background on DOS and hardware such as floppies, hard disks, modems and fax cards.

Mastering SideKick Plus
Gene Weisskopf
394pp. Ref. 558-1
Employ all of Sidekick's powerful and expanded features with this hands-on guide to the popular utility. Features include comprehensive and detailed coverage of time management, note taking, outlining, auto dialing, DOS file management, math, and copy-and-paste functions.

Norton Utilities 5 Instant Reference
Michael Gross
162pp. Ref. 737-1
Organized alphabetically by program name, this pocket-sized reference offers complete information on each utility in the Norton 5 package—including a descriptive summary, exact syntax, command line options, brief explanation, and examples. Gives proficient users a quick reminder, and helps with unfamiliar options.

PC Tools Deluxe 6 Instant Reference
Gordon McComb
194pp. Ref. 728-2
Keep this one handy for fast access to quick reminders and essential information on the latest PC Tools Utilities. Alphabetical entries cover all the Tools of Version 6—from data recovery to desktop applications—with concise summaries, syntax, options, brief explanations, and examples.

Up & Running with Carbon Copy Plus
Marvin Bryan
124pp. Ref. 709-6
A speedy, thorough introduction to Car-

bon Copy Plus, for controlling remote computers from a PC. Coverage is in twenty time-coded "steps"—lessons that take 15 minutes to an hour to complete. Topics include program set-up, making and receiving calls, file transfer, security, terminal emulation, and using Scripts.

Up & Running with Norton Utilities
Rainer Bartel
140pp. Ref. 659-6
Get up and running in the shortest possible time in just 20 lessons or "steps." Learn to restore disks and files, use UnErase, edit your floppy disks, retrieve lost data and more. Or use the book to evaluate the software before you purchase. Through Version 4.2.

Up & Running with Norton Utilities 5
Michael Gross
154pp. Ref. 819-0
Get a fast jump on Norton Utilties 5. In just 20 lessons, you can learn to retrieve erased files, password protect and encrypt your data, make your system work faster, unformat accidentally formatted disks, find "lost" files on your hard disk, and reconstruct damaged files.

Up & Running with PC Tools Deluxe 6
Thomas Holste
180pp. Ref.678-2
Learn to use this software program in just 20 basic steps. Readers get a quick, inexpensive introduction to using the Tools for disaster recovery, disk and file management, and more.

Up & Running with XTreeGold 2
Robin Merrin
136pp. Ref. 820-3
Covers both XTreeGold 2 and XTreePro-Gold 1. In just 20 steps, each taking no more than 15 minutes to an hour, you can learn to customize your display, archive files, navigate the user interface, copy and back up your files, undelete accidentally erased files, and more.

OPERATING SYSTEMS

The ABC's of DOS 4
Alan R. Miller
275pp. Ref. 583-2
This step-by-step introduction to using DOS 4 is written especially for beginners. Filled with simple examples, *The ABC's of DOS 4* covers the basics of hardware, software, disks, the system editor EDLIN, DOS commands, and more.

The ABC's of DOS 5
Alan Miller
267pp. Ref. 770-3
This straightforward guide will haven even first-time computer users working comfortably with DOS 5 in no time. Step-by-step lessons lead users from switching on the PC, through exploring the DOS Shell, working with directories and files, using essential commands, customizing the system, and trouble shooting. Includes a tear-out quick reference card and function key template.

ABC's of MS-DOS (Second Edition)
Alan R. Miller
233pp. Ref. 493-3
This handy guide to MS-DOS is all many PC users need to manage their computer files, organize floppy and hard disks, use EDLIN, and keep their computers organized. Additional information is given about utilities like Sidekick, and there is a DOS command and program summary. The second edition is fully updated for Version 3.3.

The ABC's of SCO UNIX
Tom Cuthbertson
263pp. Re. 715-0
A guide especially for beginners who want to get to work fast. Includes hands-on tutorials on logging in and out; creating and editing files; using electronic mail; organizing files into directories; printing; text formatting; and more.

The ABC's of Windows 3.0
Kris Jamsa
327pp. Ref. 760-6

A user-friendly introduction to the essentials of Windows 3.0. Presented in 64 short lessons. Beginners start with lesson one, while more advanced readers can skip ahead. Learn to use File Manager, the accessory programs, customization features, Program Manager, and more.

DESQview Instant Reference
Paul J. Perry
175pp. Ref. 809-2

This complete quick-reference command guide covers version 2.3 and DESQview 386, as well as QEMM (for managing expanded memory) and Manifest Memory Analyzer. Concise, alphabetized entries provide exact syntax, options, usage, and brief examples for every command. A handy source for on-the-job reminders and tips.

DOS 3.3 On-Line Advisor Version 1.1
SYBAR, Software Division of SYBEX, Inc.
Ref. 933-1

The answer to all your DOS problems. The DOS On-Line Advisor is an on-screen reference that explains over 200 DOS error messages. 2300 other citations cover all you ever needed to know about DOS. The DOS On-Line Advisor pops up on top of your working program to give you quick, easy help when you need it, and disappears when you don't. Covers thru version 3.3. Software package comes with 3½'' and 5¼'' disks. **System Requirements:** IBM compatible with DOS 2.0 or higher, runs with Windows 3.0, uses 90K of RAM.

DOS Instant Reference SYBEX Prompter Series
Greg Harvey
Kay Yarborough Nelson
220pp. Ref. 477-1

A complete fingertip reference for fast, easy on-line help:command summaries, syntax, usage and error messages. Organized by function—system commands, file commands, disk management, directories, batch files, I/O, networking, programming, and more. Through Version 3.3.

DOS 5 Instant Reference
Robert M. Thomas
200pp. Ref. 804-1

The comprehensive quick guide to DOS—all its features, commands, options, and versions—now including DOS 5, with the new graphical interface. Concise, alphabetized command entries provide exact syntax, options, usage, brief examples, and applicable version numbers. Fully cross-referenced; ideal for quick review or on-the-job reference.

The DOS 5 User's Handbook
Gary Masters
Richard Allen King
400pp. Ref. 777-0

This is the DOS 5 book for users who are already familiar with an earlier version of DOS. Part I is a quick, friendly guide to new features; topics include the graphical interface, new and enhanced commands, and much more. Part II is a complete DOS 5 quick reference, with command summaries, in-depth explanations, and examples.

Encyclopedia DOS
Judd Robbins
1030pp. Ref. 699-5

A comprehensive reference and user's guide to all versions of DOS through 4.0. Offers complete information on every DOS command, with all possible switches and parameters—plus examples of effective usage. An invaluable tool.

Essential OS/2 (Second Edition)
Judd Robbins
445pp. Ref. 609-X

Written by an OS/2 expert, this is the guide to the powerful new resources of the OS/2 operating system standard edition 1.1 with presentation manager. Robbins introduces the standard edition, and details multitasking under OS/2, and the range of commands for installing, starting up, configuring, and running applications. For Version 1.1 Standard Edition.

Essential PC-DOS (Second Edition)
Myril Clement Shaw
Susan Soltis Shaw
332pp. Ref. 413-5

An authoritative guide to PC-DOS, including version 3.2. Designed to make experts out of beginners, it explores everything from disk management to batch file programming. Includes an 85-page command summary. Through Version 3.2.

Graphics Programming Under Windows
Brian Myers
Chris Doner
646pp. Ref. 448-8

Straightforward discussion, abundant examples, and a concise reference guide to graphics commands make this book a must for Windows programmers. Topics range from how Windows works to programming for business, animation, CAD, and desktop publishing. For Version 2.

Hard Disk Instant Reference SYBEX Prompter Series
Judd Robbins
256pp. Ref. 587-5

Compact yet comprehensive, this pocket-sized reference presents the essential information on DOS commands used in managing directories and files, and in optimizing disk configuration. Includes a survey of third-party utility capabilities. Through DOS 4.0.

Inside DOS: A Programmer's Guide
Michael J. Young
490pp. Ref. 710-X

A collection of practical techniques (with source code listings) designed to help you take advantage of the rich resources intrinsic to MS-DOS machines. Designed for the experienced programmer with a basic

understanding of C and 8086 assembly language, and DOS fundamentals.

Mastering DOS (Second Edition)
Judd Robbins
722pp. Ref. 555-7

"The most useful DOS book." This seven-part, in-depth tutorial addresses the needs of users at all levels. Topics range from running applications, to managing files and directories, configuring the system, batch file programming, and techniques for system developers. Through Version 4.

Mastering DOS 5
Judd Robbins
800pp. Ref.767-3

"The DOS reference to keep next to your computer," according to PC Week, this highly acclaimed text is now revised and expanded for DOS 5. Comprehensive tutorials cover everything from first steps for beginners, to advanced tools for systems developers—with emphasis on the new graphics interface. Includes tips, tricks, and a tear-out quick reference card and function key template.

Mastering SunOS
Brent D. Heslop
David Angell
588pp. Ref. 683-9

Learn to configure and manage your system; use essential commands; manage files; perform editing, formatting, and printing tasks; master E-mail and external communication; and use the SunView and new Open Window graphic interfaces.

Mastering Windows 3.0
Robert Cowart
592pp. Ref.458-5

Every Windows user will find valuable how-to and reference information here. With full details on the desktop utilities; manipulating files; running applications (including non-Windows programs); sharing data between DOS, OS/2, and Windows; hardware and software efficiency tips; and more.

Understanding DOS 3.3
Judd Robbins
678pp. Ref. 648-0

This best selling, in-depth tutorial addresses the needs of users at all levels with many examples and hands-on exercises. Robbins discusses the fundamentals of DOS, then covers manipulating files and directories, using the DOS editor, printing, communicating, and finishes with a full section on batch files.

Understanding Hard Disk Management on the PC
Jonathan Kamin
500pp. Ref. 561-1

This title is a key productivity tool for all hard disk users who want efficient, error-free file management and organization. Includes details on the best ways to conserve hard disk space when using several memory-guzzling programs. Through DOS 4.

Up & Running with DR DOS 5.0
Joerg Schieb
130pp. Ref. 815-7

Enjoy a fast-paced, but thorough introduction to DR DOS 5.0. In only 20 steps, you can begin to obtain practical results: copy and delete files, password protect your data, use batch files to save time, and more.

Up & Running with DOS 3.3
Michael-Alexander Beisecker
126pp. Ref. 750-9

Learn the fundamentals of DOS 3.3 in just 20 basic steps. Each "step" is a self-contained, time-coded lesson, taking 15 minutes to an hour to complete. You learn the essentials in record time.

Up & Running with DOS 5
Alan Simpson
150pp. Ref. 774-6

A 20-step guide to the essentials of DOS 5—for busy users seeking a fast-paced overview. Steps take only minutes to complete, and each is marked with a timer clock, so you know how long each one will take. Topics include installation, the DOS Shell, Program Manager, disks, directories, utilities, customization, batch files, ports and devices, DOSKEY, memory, Windows, and BASIC.

Up & Running with Your Hard Disk
Klaus M Rubsam
140pp. Ref. 666-9

A far-sighted, compact introduction to hard disk installation and basic DOS use. Perfect for PC users who want the practical essentials in the shortest possible time. In 20 basic steps, learn to choose your hard disk, work with accessories, back up data, use DOS utilities to save time, and more.

Up & Running with Windows 286/386
Gabriele Wentges
132pp. Ref. 691-X

This handy 20-step overview gives PC users all the essentials of using Windows—whether for evaluating the software, or getting a fast start. Each self-contained lesson takes just 15 minutes to one hour to complete.